# THE GOWN AND THE GAVEL

# THE GOWN AND THE GAVEL

LIFE JOURNEY OF A
FORMER CHIEF JUSTICE OF INDIA

G.B. PATNAIK

PAPER MISSILE

NIYOGI
BOOKS

Published by
NIYOGI BOOKS
Block D, Building No. 77,
Okhla Industrial Area, Phase-I,
New Delhi-110 020, INDIA
Tel: 011-26818960, +91 7428978881
Email: niyogibooks@gmail.com
Website: www.niyogibooksindia.com



Editor: Anwesha Panda
Design: Shashi Bhushan Prasad

ISBN: 978-81-19626-78-6
Publication: 2025

Every effort has been made to ensure the accuracy of the information presented in this book. The images used in this book come from either the public domain or from the public commons, unless otherwise stated.



Printed at Niyogi Offset Pvt. Ltd., New Delhi, India

*For my grandsons*
*Aaryaman, Ayushman and Devansh*

# Contents

# Foreword

Writing a judgment is hard; writing an autobiography at the age of 86 after more than two decades of retirement as Chief Justice of India is even harder. In 2021, Justice G.B. Patnaik penned his autobiography in Odia. He has done it again, writing his autobiography in English explaining in clear prose his journey from early upbringing in a small Odisha village to his present retired life as a senior citizen.

One of our distinguished and highly experienced judicial minds, he has written an account that covers his childhood memories of an 'inauspicious house' in the village to his legal journey that started in Cuttack initially in the office of senior advocate Mr. B.K. Pal and then with Barrister B.M. Patnaik, which was quite rewarding before he joined the office of the advocate general as a standing counsel/government advocate where he had a tenure of about 11 years. It was during this time that due to his hard work and effective advocacy, he came in close contact with the top bureaucracy of the state of Odisha and its chief ministers.

At the time of his first recommendation for the high court judgeship in 1979, he was less than 45 years of age. The name of Justice G.B. Patnaik was recommended based solely on merit and as a man of good character. He was a teetotaler then. However, a section of the Cuttack Bar was hell bent upon forestalling his appointment. Some lawyers being part of that group met the then Prime Minister Mr Morarji Desai and impressed upon him that Mr G.B. Patnaik was a young man addicted to drinks as well as a womaniser. Mr Morarji Desai was a staunch pro-prohibition man and ensured through the law minister that CJI withdrew his name.

It is indeed unthinkable that in a democracy governed by rule of law and the constitutional provisions and processes, the Prime Minister should act in a most arbitrary manner over the interests of the individual. Every action of the Prime Minister must be informed with reason and be free from arbitrariness. That is the essence of good governance and fairness. The process of appointment of high judicial office is no exception. This incident changed Justice G.B. Patnaik and he became a social drinker. Hurdles can be put in someone's way of progression but destiny cannot be blocked. He was destined to adorn high judicial office and within 4 years of the initial setback, he was elevated as a judge of the Orissa High Court.

Elevation and transfer of judges have always been shrouded in mystery. This was called 'court management' by the then Chief Justice of India R.S. Pathak, when as a junior judge in Orissa High Court, Justice G.B. Patnaik asked him, how was it that at a given point of time there could be three persons from one high court being appointed as Chief Justices of different high courts, while there would be none from some high courts. Interestingly, this system of 'court management' continues even after the collegium system has been put in place.

I came to the Supreme Court much after he had retired as Chief Justice of India and therefore, I had no occasion to work with him in the Supreme Court. However, after my retirement, both of us were associated in two arbitration matters, one matter in which he was the presiding arbitrator and the other, where I was the presiding arbitrator. In both matters, his guidance had been invaluable.

The story of one of the most veteran judges in the country, it is a treat for anyone who is interested in peering into an inspiring story of a village boy who became the Chief Justice of India.

Justice R.M. Lodha
Former Chief Justice of India

# Preface

On 26 November 2021, in course of releasing my autobiography in Odia, titled *Mane Achhi Jetiki*, Dr Murlidhar, the then Chief Justice of Orissa High Court, had expressed that the book should be translated in English so that people throughout the country would have the opportunity of reading the same. My friend Anant Mahapatra, on whose persuasion and insistence I had written my autobiography in Odia, came forward to help me get the book translated into English. But I told him that if at all I ever think of having an English version, I would write one myself rather than get the Odia version translated. I toyed with the idea for about a year, and during that period some of my friends, after going through the Odia book, sent some suggestions for improvement. I also realised that my two grandsons who grew up in Germany, Aryaman and Aayushman, really want to go through my autobiography but are incapable of reading the Odia language. Thus, I decided to start writing my biography in English, which is not a translation from the Odia but an entirely new version, though the essential components remain unchanged.

I have organised my life story into 9 chapters, each chapter being relatable to one period of life, starting with my childhood spent in my ancestral village in Odisha and culminating in a retired life in the city of Delhi. This book serves as a record of my journey from being a wide-eyed medical college aspirant wanting to do good in society to embracing the legal profession, fully aware of uncertainties that awaited me, particularly as a first-generation lawyer lacking connections or financial support. As a young lawyer, the path was no doubt challenging but navigable through honesty, sincerity and integrity. In the course of my legal stint, my name was even considered for judgeship at the young age of 41, though my dreams were thwarted due to external interference and machinations. Surprisingly, the same person who opposed my elevation later suggested my name for the very same position. This led me to believe that destiny plays a crucial role, but one should not passively wait for fate to unfold. My own life disproves the societal perception that even today in the Indian judicial system only the children of judges ascend to positions in the higher judiciary.

In the pages of this book, I have recounted memorable incidents and interesting cases without revealing names, striving to dispel long-held misconceptions about the Indian judiciary and convey unpalatable truths without the intent to humiliate. The narrative also delves into my reflections on the country's governance and the challenges faced by the common man. I believe that the Constitution of India allows every citizen in the country to express their opinion freely. I am hopeful the book will instil confidence in the minds of young law graduates and encourage them to enter the legal profession, particularly one who is prepared to work hard and carry themselves with steadfast adherence to legal ethics. Let the lessons I've learned in this profession guide you through life, dear readers.

I started the project of writing this book in mid-2022 and could conclude the same only by July 2023. When I had written my biography in Odia, I had to write in long hand, which was a very tough task. But when I started my English version, it became easier, as I would dictate to my secretary, Gaurav Parashar, and correct the proofs later. Gaurav not only assisted in transcribing the dictation but also provided printouts, reprinted after corrections, including those made by Prof. Himanshu Mahapatra, who initiated the task. As the book expanded, I sought advice from a friend, Nirmal Kanti Bhattacharya, who suggested the name of an editor, Upama Biswas, to take on the responsibility of editing and streamlining the content.

I take this opportunity to express my heartfelt gratitude to my childhood friend Anant Mahapatra, who consistently encouraged me to finish the book. I also extend my thanks to J.P. Das, an eminent writer and good friend, for his valuable suggestions during our discussions. I thank my family, friends and well-wishers who, after reviewing the Odia version, provided suggestions that I have faithfully incorporated into this English rendition of my biography. Professor Himanshu Mahapatra's initial corrections were crucial, and I appreciate his efforts. Special thanks goes out to Gaurav Parashar, without whom it would not have been possible to accomplish this monumental task. Upama Biswas deserves thanks for her dedicated editing, making valuable alterations while preserving the substantial structure of the book. And last but not the least, my gratitude to Niyogi Books for agreeing to publish this work.

# Childhood and Village

The mighty Kalinga Empire of yore underwent dismemberment during British Rule and lost its former independent identity. Its eastern and northern parts got incorporated into the Calcutta Presidency, while the southern and western parts were incorporated into the Madras Presidency and Central Provinces and Berar, respectively, leaving aside 26 states ruled by independent rulers. In 1911, Bihar and Orissa were conjoined to form a separate province. Our forefathers fought with the British administration to make Orissa a separate province that would comprise all the Odia-speaking tracts, and as a result, the British administration declared Orissa as a separate province with effect from 1 April 1936.

I was born a year later, on 19 December 1937, in the newly declared province of Orissa, the place of my birth being 'Makaram Manzil', a house situated in the Oriya Bazaar locality in Cuttack where my father lived on rent after he had returned from Patna. A month or so after my birth, my father shifted to a newly constructed house in the same neighbourhood. The house in question was opposite to Janakinath Bhawan, the ancestral house of the Bose family, where Netaji Subhash Chandra Bose was born. The house remained our residence till 1969, except for a gap of about two years during which time my father's office was shifted to Sambalpur. It is from this house that my father became a gazetted officer in the Orissa secretariat and retired as undersecretary in the finance department of the Government of Orissa. It is here that my uncle Braja Behari got married. It is from this house that I completed my student career and started practising law in Orissa High Court. I even spent the early years of my married life in this house, and it is where my eldest son Amar was born.

Though I spent a substantial part of my life in this house, the superstitious belief of being inauspicious shrouded me. A few months after my family shifted to this house, my elder brother, who was just three years old, suddenly passed away, leading our neighbours to tell my mother that the house was an inauspicious one. It is with this indoctrinated belief that my mother apparently sold me to a Muslim family for a sum of two annas and re-purchased me by paying two rupees after a couple of years. I never believed the house to be inauspicious and what I have narrated is proof of my belief. There were five rooms with a long veranda, a kitchen and a small courtyard. However, the rooms were very small. When we received more guests, the veranda was used as a bedroom, and during summer, the terrace was the usual place to sleep. There was no electricity or tap water connection. I remember how my uncle and I used to fetch drinking water from a distant tubewell at night. The initials of my father's name, Rash Behari Patnaik, RBP, was imprinted on the door, and it remained there long after we left the house in 1969, standing testament to many years spent there.

In the district of Puri, under Delanga PS, there is a village named Ghorodia, about 8 km from Delanga railway station and about 6 km from the village Beraboi, where Mahatma Gandhi held camp in 1934 when he was touring Orissa. In the said village, Narayan and Antaryami, my grandfather, were the two sons of Dinabandhu. Dinabandhu's brother was Madhava. As

Madhava had no heir, he adopted Antaryami. Antaryami had four sons and four daughters, while his elder brother Narayan had six sons and two daughters. These two brothers and their children and grandchildren constituted a Hindu joint family, which was known as 'Das Family'. At that time, even though a middle-class family, our family was considered the most influential one in the area, with agricultural land going up to 80 acres, an 8-acre orchard and the homestead spread over more than 2 acres. The entire family, consisting of more than 50–60 people, depended on the produce from the agricultural land, though some of the children of Narayan and Antaryami were in government service.

Narayan used to manage the family property, and Antaryami used to work as a higher-grade pleader's clerk in Puri. He was not only attached to a pleader's office but could also plead himself as 'Degreedhari Moharir', probably something like a *mukhtar*, and would argue before different courts in revenue matters. From the latter's earnings rose a two-storeyed pucca building consisting of eight rooms, and another eight–ten thatched rooms at the back of the main house with a large vacant area behind, which together constituted the homestead of Das family. An interesting fact is that while our family name was 'Das', my grandfather had changed his surname to 'Patnaik', though the reason is still a mystery, so Antaryami's children came to bear the surname Patnaik.

Golakh Behari, the eldest son of Antaryami, was a police inspector and died at a very young age. Antaryami's second son, Rash Behari, my father, was to appear for his matriculation in the Puri Zilla School when his father died. Having completed his matriculation, he moved to Cuttack for his higher studies and joined Intermediate in Arts at the Ravenshaw College. He appeared for the said examination but could not clear it. Hence, at a very young age, he left for Ranchi in Bihar to earn a living, where he was appointed as an assistant clerk in the office of the accountant general. I think he did not take a second chance possibly because both his father and his elder brother had passed away, and the family was solely dependent on the usufruct of the agricultural land of the joint family. Having continued in the office of the accountant general for a couple of years, he got appointed as lower division clerk in the office of the commissioner of Income Tax at Patna. He continued in the same post till 1936, when Orissa was declared as a separate province, and he was absorbed as a clerk in the finance department under the Government of Orissa. During that period, our family consisted of my father and mother, my eldest sister, a brother, my grandmother and my uncle Bana Behari. Another brother of mine had died a couple of days after being born when my father was at Ranchi.

My father's younger brother, Braja Behari, was a brilliant student throughout his school days, and even received scholarships for his higher education. He always stood first in all examinations, starting from middle class till he obtained his MSc degree. After Independence, he went to England and obtained his PhD from University of Leeds. On his return to India in early 1949, he started living with us in Oriya Bazar. I remember, he had brought with him a Bush radio from England, and since there was no electricity, the radio operated on battery. He was appointed as a senior scientific officer in Defence Research and Development Organisation (DRDO) under the Ministry of Defence and left for Delhi in 1950. I remember the party held on the terrace of our Oriya Bazar house, which was attended by a galaxy of educationists, including Dr P.K. Parija and Dr B. Prasad, among others. He retired as the director of DRDO, a position which no other Odia person had achieved at that point of time.

My youngest uncle, Bana Behari, was an idle kind and had become a bit wayward. My father took him to Patna with him in the hope that he would pursue some profession. However, it was all in vain. My father contemplated that he was too old to mend his ways. When the Secretariat was shifted to Sambalpur, my father got him appointed as assistant caretaker. There he learnt typing. When the Secretariat was shifted back to Cuttack, he was appointed as a typist in the law department. Finally, he retired as head typist.

Our village Ghorodia was a long stretch of more than two miles, and on one side there was the village school and on the other side there was the River Daya. The villagers were mostly agrarians, though a few had other occupations. There were two temples, one of Lord Radhakanth Dev, which was right in front of our house, and the other of Lord Radha Mohan Dev, which was by the riverside. These two deities were prominent institutions in the village, and the manager of both the institutions had a great influence on the villagers and their affairs. My grandfather's brother, Narayan, managed the property of the temple trust of Lord Radhakanth Dev. I still remember several functions of Lord Radhakanth Dev being performed with grandeur. As a four-year-old, I was taken to the temple to perform the ceremony called *karnavedha*, which is usually performed between the first and fifth year of a child's life, a spiritual and symbolic ceremony marking the beginning of the child's learning in life. The only thing I remember is that one of my father's cousins took me on his lap and pierced my earlobe. A handful of *chhena* or cottage cheese and banana paste was forcibly put into my mouth to prevent me from crying. My father had performed the ceremony with much pomp, and many important members of the village were also invited for lunch within the temple precinct. This was in the year 1941.

In 1942, back in our Oriya Bazaar residence, I started learning in a *chatsala*, which was right in front of our house. The Second World War was already in progress. Apprehending the possibility of an attack by German forces on Cuttack town, the Government of Orissa shifted the secretariat to Sambalpur, and therefore, my father went to Sambalpur along with my uncle Bana Behari. My mother, along with me, my sister and younger brother, went to our maternal uncle's house in a village named Naragang, under Banki PS, in Cuttack district. There we welcomed my younger brother, who was later named Jagat. Later on, he was adopted by my maternal uncle since he had no heir. My maternal grandfather, Satyabadi Patnaik, who had been conferred with the title of 'Bebarta' by the Raja of Banki, was a landlord with a vast amount of agricultural land. The Bebarta family was a well-known family in the area and collected revenues from two–three villages. My uncle had a house in each of those villages, which he enjoyed till the enactment of Odisha Estate Abolition Act of 1952. However, his house was not as impressive when compared to our ancestral house in Ghorodia. We lived there for about seven–eight months. I started attending the first standard lessons at the village school that my uncle had started. I learnt much later that my name was the maiden one to be registered.

I spent a couple of my early years (1942 and 1943) in our ancestral house in Ghorodia, studying in class II and III at the village school, where one could study up to class V. This was the only educational institution in the whole village with a population of around 4,000–5,000 people. Then came the partition of our joint family, with the family property divided into two shares, one for the heirs of Narayan and the other for the heirs of Antaryami. As far as Antaryami's share was concerned, the heirs were my father, his two brothers and the widow of Golakh Behari. In 1944, since my grandmother was still staying at the village house and was not in the condition to move to Cuttack, my mother, my eldest sister as well as my younger brother stayed behind with her, while I was sent to live with my father in Cuttack.

Having spent two years in my village and thereafter each holiday in my village, as my mother continued to stay there till 1951, I developed a strong affinity towards my village and more particularly for Lord Radhakanth Dev. Two years of my village life had a strong impact on me as a child. It was reflected in the fact that when I joined school in Cuttack,

I thought of pursuing medicine and starting my private practice either in the village or in the nearby semi-urban place near Khurda Road, which is a major railway junction and has a large population. I wanted to serve the local people of my village; I even resolved to become a representative to the Legislative Assembly so that I could make a difference. The idea was to create an atmosphere of development in the village and live a simple and rustic life.

With time, my visits to my village also dwindled. But when my uncle Bana Behari started living in our village after his retirement, I began visiting my ancestral house at least two–three times a year. Even today, the village does not have the modern amenities that I had envisioned. The old kutcha road has been converted to a pucca road and the village now has electricity and water supply, but there is neither any healthcare facility nor a bank. The majority of the villagers are barely educated, though there exists a high school in the village. Open defecation still continues. Although now there are more shops catering to the daily needs of the villagers. The only substantial change that has taken place is that most of the houses that were once thatched have become pucca buildings. However, our ancestral double-storey building that once stood tall is in a dilapidated condition today. In fact, it is one of my great disappointments in life that even after reaching the highest position in the judicial hierarchy of the country, I could not maintain the house that my grandfather had built on the earning of a pleader's clerk, despite his short lifespan.

# School Life at Cuttack

My father had decided that I would continue my schooling after class III in Cuttack. This was in spite of my mother staying back in our village with my grandmother and there being no other female member in our Oriya Bazaar house. So, in June 1944, only seven years old, I left my village with Uncle Bana Behari and headed to Cuttack. I still vividly remember us travelling the distance from my village to the nearest railway station at Delang, which was about 8 km, by bullock cart and boarding the Puri–Talcher Passenger Train. Though it was my first experience of travelling by train and I was in awe of the entire experience, I didn't enjoy it as much, as I missed my mother.

We reached the Cuttack station around 6 in the evening. A new chapter in my life was about to begin. Outside the station we saw horse carriages and hand-pulled rickshaws, which were the only mode of public transport back then. We hired a rickshaw to take us to our house in Oriya Bazar. My father, uncle and three other male relatives stayed in that house besides a cook and a young boy hired to clean the house. That night my father had himself cooked some special dishes for my arrival. I had my dinner with him and went to bed tired after a very hectic day.

The nearest high school was Peary Mohan Academy, and Mr Basant Kumar Das was the headmaster. I was to appear for an interview with the headmaster for my admission, therefore my father coached me every evening after returning from work. On the date fixed for the purpose, I went with my father to the school, which was a ten-minute walk from home. We sat outside the headmaster's office waiting to be called in. I was nervous and sat in silence, not exchanging a word with my father. As soon as my name was called, I entered the headmaster's room with much apprehension. My father also entered the room and took a seat. The headmaster then called me to his side, put his hand on my shoulder and started to question me. What would be the English word for *bhala*, he asked in Odia. Upon my saying 'good', he thanked me and asked what would be the opposite word of 'good', and I immediately said 'Bad.' The headmaster said, 'Very good!' Then he asked me, 'Are you a bad boy?' I said, 'Yes, Sir.' Amused, he told me, 'You probably gave the wrong answer,' and then proceeded to write on my application 'Admit'. He told my father to deposit the necessary fees in the office and that classes would start in a week's time. My father then deposited the fees and we both headed home. On the way, though, my father scolded me for giving the wrong answer to the last question. During that one-week period, everybody from our house would leave for work, including our cook, who was also peon in the supply department. I, left to myself the whole day, would feel home sick and cry, remembering my mother.

On the first day of school, I found myself assigned to the 'A' section. Every class consisted of two sections, and in each section, there were about 40 students. A couple of students were also staying in the hostel, as they came from far away villages, and wore dhoti and shirt to school. There were no uniforms or prescribed 'school dress' as we'd call them back then, and the usual outfit was a half-pant (shorts) and a half-sleeve shirt, so a tailor named Umar, who had a shop near our house, stitched four half-pants and four half-shirts for me and delivered them within a couple of days.

Gradually, I got accustomed to life as a student in Cuttack. I still remember how my father took care of me those days, not only giving me a bath but also getting me fed and ready for school. School was from 10 am to 4 pm with a single recess at noon. Though some children did eat a snack brought from home, I enjoyed my break playing with my friends in the school compound. Coming back from school at 4 pm, I would leave my books at home by slipping them through a little opening in the locked front door, since everybody was still at work. I would then rush back to the school playground to play and only return before dark. By the time I would return, our cook would have returned. He would make me a sumptuous snack, as that was my first big meal since breakfast. My father used to return from the office by 7 pm and would sit down with me for lessons every evening for two hours. He was very good in English, and as a result, I scored the highest marks in the subject.

The first period in class began with a prayer "*Raghu Pati Raghav Raja Ram-Patita Pavan Sita Ram*". Once a week, there used to be a class in which spinning thread out of cotton was taught. Nobody under the British administration had ever objected to such a curriculum. But today, in Independent India, notwithstanding its secular stance, with no state religion and diversity of culture, a government order in the state of Karnataka prohibiting girls wearing the hijab to enter into school created a row not only in the said state but disturbed other states too. As of May 2024, the high court is hearing a public interest litigation to decide whether the practice of putting on a hijab is an individual's right to practise the religion and whether the right of the state government to impose a dress code in a government educational institution is arbitrary or irrational. It cannot be denied that our country is a multi-cultural, multi-religious society with a young and vibrant population. This puts the onus on leaders and politicians to motivate the youth and look for ways to unite rather than divide our people. And the courts these days, sadly, remain busy in deciding such issues, often doing what the government should do.

In school, one of the most-awaited events was the annual picnic, and the month of December was the preferred time generally. Our school annual picnic used to be at nearby places where we could go in the morning and come back by evening. The contribution used to be only 8 annas or 1 rupee. It was in class VIII that we had our first long excursion of four days to Bhubaneshwar accompanied by our class teacher, Mr Ganeswar Praharaj. Getting down from the train at the railway station, we walked to a *dharamsala* near Lingaraj Temple where we were to put up. We spent the days going around the town, stopping particularly at the historic places. What I found most impressive was our visit to Dhauli, the site of the Kalinga War, fought between the feudal kingdom of Kalinga and the Mauryan Empire under the leadership of Ashoka the Great. It was considered one of the deadliest battles to be fought in Indian history. We were also taken to Rajarani Temple, an 11th-century Hindu temple with exquisite architecture and carvings. These two were besides several other places of interest visited. Another memorable excursion was to Jamshedpur when I was in class X. We were accompanied by our headmaster and our senior-most teacher. As far as I remember, we were a group of about 50 students on this trip. As there was no direct train, we went by train from Cuttack to Kharagpur, and changed trains to reach Jamshedpur early next morning. As we got off the train, the entire sky looked red as if the sun had just risen, but actually the colour was due to molten slag being dumped at the dumping yard. Jamshedpur was where India's first iron and steel plant was set up in 1908 by Jamshedji Nusserwanji Tata, the Parsi industrialist. We were in Jamshedpur for three days, and for two days, we visited the TISCO (Tata Iron and Steel Company) factory and were excited to observe the process of steel manufacturing. The city was cleaner and much well-organised compared to Cuttack. The friends who, I remember, accompanied me on this memorable trip were Saroj Patnaik, Sunil Patnaik, Manoranjan Patnaik and Bipin Mahapatra.

I often sit back and remember my old friends and the happy times we spent together. My best friend in school was a village lad named Gourmohan, a brilliant student, with whom I reconnected at the school reunion in 2003–04 and stayed in touch since till he passed away in 2021. Among my later friends were Sourindra Bose, Shakti Das Mukherjee, Sovan Kanungo, Sarada Prasad Mohanty and Ravi Patnaik. Sourindra and Shakti were also from the same locality as mine, and we used to go to school together and return together. Another friend that comes to mind was Jitendrya Sarangi, who used to stand either first or second in our section.

I remember a happy incident from 1952 when I finished school, and my good friend Sovan Kanungo decided to pursue his higher studies in Delhi, as his father was by then a Member of Parliament (MP) and staying in Delhi. I thought of throwing a small party in his honour with a bunch of other close friends. Such a thing was unheard of in those days, and my father was not in favour of the idea, as he thought it would not be appropriate to invite a rich man's son to our house. That was the first occasion when I realised socio-economic hierarchy exists—that there was a difference between a rich man's son and the son of a middle-class family, though they may be studying together in the same class and school. This manmade social stratification never affected our innocent minds at school; for the eight years we studied together, never had such feelings come to my mind. My friends and I shared a bond of mutual affection. Sovan's behaviour was always cordial and he showed great personal regard for his friends. When I invited him to the party, he accepted the invitation so gladly, I cannot now describe the excitement and glow I saw on his face that day.

It was a Sunday evening. My father, my mother and our cook got together to prepare a number of delicacies for the evening. Sweet dishes were purchased from the local sweet shop. The rooftop where we would have dinner was fully cleaned and, in the evening, a petromax light was brought on rent, as we had no electricity in our house. The party started at 7 in the evening and ended at 10 in the night, with my father supervising the management of guests. This was the only occasion in the eight years of school life when I got the opportunity to call my friends home for a party. Today my grandsons probably have a party in school every month on the occasion of some or the other friend's birthday. How times have changed not only with our food and dress but also with our daily habits.

A global conflict that played out in my youth and had a lasting impression on my mind was the events of the Second World War. Deemed the deadliest conflict in human history, it involved virtually every part of the world. Though fought predominantly in Europe, it involved personnel from almost 30 nations and resulted in around 80 million fatalities. India then being a part of the British Empire played its part in the form of sending soldiers to the war besides being a large production centre of war supplies like shoes, uniforms, parachutes, etc. In fact, Japanese forces had advanced to India's North East borders attempting to take control of the Allied forces' supply bases there. Orissa being in the east of India was always on red alert. I still remember the sirens when military planes flew overhead, and we were instructed to take refuge in our homes and close every door and window and wait in silence till we were allowed to open up again. I was in class V when the War finally ended on 8 May 1945. There were victory celebrations in school and also at home. Not only was school closed for three days, people also distributed sweets.

Then came 15 August 1947. The celebrations after India gained independence from British rule were distinct form that when the War ended in that they were spontaneous and optimistic. I still recollect the enthusiasm and zeal with which I had decorated our Oriya Bazaar house all on my own. As the offices were closed, my father had left for our village, and only my uncle Bana Behari and the cook were there. The whole week was free for me, different programmes were being organised within and outside the school campus to commemorate the day. I remember visiting the Ravenshaw College playground to watch a football match. I participated in a debate competition organised at the town hall in Cuttack. In school, too, there were celebrations, besides the distribution of sweets. There were lectures delivered by our teachers, and they painted a very bright future for our young nation, full of hope and prosperity.

Every citizen dreamt of development, equal opportunities, employment and eradication of hunger and poverty. The common man hoped for a reasonably comfortable life, a house for himself and his family, education for his children and basic healthcare. In retrospect, though, I think none of those dreams were ever fully realised. Though we have completed 75 years of Independence, India's social and economic aspirations have largely remined unfulfilled. Every citizen is still not assured of one square meal per day. It is true that the country became free from British rule and became known as an independent republic, where citizens have the right to freedom of speech guaranteed by the Constitution of India. But are these rights absolute? I have my reservations. Criticism and objection are not wilfully accepted, and efforts are often made to quash rebellion, like the declaration of Emergency in 1975 or more recently the abrogation of Article 370 in Kashmir and the negation of special status to Jammu and Kashmir. Jawaharlal Nehru, an ardent freedom fighter and the first PM of free India, had said in his "Freedom at Midnight" speech at the Red Fort in 1947 that, 'As long as there are tears and suffering, so long our work will not be over,' and it still isn't.

The death of Mahatma Gandhi in 1948 was yet another landmark event in my childhood. It was a cold winter evening when we received the message while playing in the school playground. While walking home that evening, I noticed that all the doors to the houses in the Muslim colony were closed and only a few people were outside, who huddled together whispering amongst themselves. I reached my house, anxious and with many questions on my mind. Oriya Bazar, in fact, has a 60 per cent Muslim population, and these were the very same people who had enthusiastically celebrated India's Independence. However, not knowing who killed Gandhi, we assumed that the assailant must have been a Muslim fellow, based on the fact that severe communal riots followed India's Partition just the previous year. Though we had a house full of relatives, the mood was sombre and everyone spoke in soft voices. No one left the house that evening, and we spent the night behind closed doors fearing a backlash or riots again. The streets were desolate that night. There was no radio in our house and the only source of news was the newspaper. That evening the newspaper did not arrive, and when it did the next morning, we found that the assailant was one Nathuram Godse, a member of the Rashtriya Swayamsevak Sangh (RSS). As a young boy, I thought to myself, what an irony and gross blunder committed, assassinating the Father of the Nation, who advocated non-violence, by taking recourse to violence.

When my grandmother died in 1951, my mother came to live with us at our Oriya Bazar home. The arrival of a lady in the house brought new fervour to religious celebrations. Her presence had a profound impact on how food and rituals were observed within the household. Durga Puja was the biggest community festival celebrated together by all the residents of the area. My favourite festivals, though, were Ganesh Chaturthi and Basant Panchami, as they were also celebrated in school, and I was allowed to stay out late with friends and return home at night, unlike other days when I was expected to be home before dark.

My father was a strict disciplinarian and also got angry if my younger brother and I did not fare well in the school examinations. Incidentally, my younger brother joined the same school three years later, in 1947, in class IV. We were so scared of our father that we never discussed anything with him nor did we ever make any demand. Whatever be our needs, it was conveyed to him through our mother. However, my elder sister, who was older than us and the apple of my father's eye, was very free with him. It is from her that I learnt that my father was also a very fashionable person, fond of good food and had a sense of humour too. He apparently often used to play pranks and crack jokes with her. After the death of my elder brother, which I have mentioned earlier, his attitude towards life changed totally. This lack of communication with the children, I think in retrospect, was not conducive for me growing up. Especially when it came to career advice and educational choices.

As long as my father was teaching me at home, i.e., from class IV to VII, I stood either the second or third position in my class. But the curriculum in class VIII was such that my father was finding it difficult to tutor me, particularly arithmetic. A cousin of mine who was proficient in mathematics used to help me at home, but in the annual examination, my position in class came down to fourth and the same occurred in class IX too. It was, therefore, my father's decision to send me to a private tutor. The tutor also happened to be my class teacher, Mr Jagat Bandhu Patnaik. He gave special attention to English, and I was doing very well in my class, often securing the highest or the second-highest marks. In the class X annual examination, I secured good marks in all subjects except Sanskrit. Since the matriculation examination was fast approaching, my tutor suggested I should take coaching in Sanskrit for the next few months and I did so. In fact, my father's friend who was working in the office of the Director of Public Instruction, Orissa, arranged for a *pandit* who came for an hour every day to teach me.

The matriculation examination, which I took in February 1952, is still fresh in my mind. For the first time, the examination hall would be in a different school and the students got admit cards to sit the examination.

For the students of our school, the examination was being conducted in Ravenshaw Collegiate School, and it continued for four days everyday with two sessions. I even got eight annas every day to have a snack during the mid-day recess. When the examinations were over, my friends and I discussed the question papers and our headmaster himself speculated that at least eight of us, including me, would get the first division, a big achievement in those days.

After the matriculation examination got over in March, I had a long vacation, as the college admission process would begin in June or July. I spent my time during this period either playing cricket with friends or visiting relatives in town or outside Cuttack.

It was during this break I got a chance to make my second trip outside Orissa, this time to Calcutta, with my cousin, my father's sister's son, Late Nabakishore, who worked in the postal department and travelled with mails in trains. It was a memorable trip with visits to the Indian Museum, the Victoria Memorial, the open-air market Mangla Haat near Howrah Station, the Alipore Zoo, the Hogg Market or New Market as it is famously known, and buying sweet delicacies from K.C. Das sweet shop for my family back in Cuttack. I even rode the tram, and was awestruck by the bustling city, which was like a mammoth compared to a small town like Cuttack.

Back from Calcutta, days were dragging by and there was nothing to do except anxiously wait for the result of my matriculation examination. It was then one evening that my father told me that he would take me to spend some time with my elder sister and brother-in-law in Berhampur. This unexpected opportunity arose when the first Finance Commission of the country, with K.C. Niyogi as chairman, was visiting Orissa, and my father, as the head assistant in the finance department, was on official duty to accompany the commission to Koraput, since they wanted to see the tribal areas of the state. Berhampur was en route to Koraput, so my father could drop me off by car and then proceed to Koraput on work. So, the next day, with a small bag in hand, I left with my father in a very big car for Berhampur. Travelling by car was also a memorable event for me, since back then, car travel was a luxury. As far as I remember, a distant relative of ours, who was a barrister practising in Cuttack High Court, had a car. He used to visit our house often, and I was fascinated by his car and would look through the windows at the shining dashboard and polished seats. This trip to Berhampur was, in fact, my first experience of travelling inside a car. At my sister's place, I spent almost 10 days basking in the love and hospitality showered on me so generously. Then my brother-in-law, sister and I joined my parents on a trip to Vizag to visit the 13th-century temple dedicated to Varaha Laxmi Narasimha, an incarnation of God Vishnu, built on the Simhachalam Hills. The temple was considered an important religious site, just like the Jagannath Temple in Puri.

But once back home, I spent my time roaming the city of Cuttack on cycle along with my friends and playing cricket for all afternoon. Few days thereafter, the matriculation examination results were declared. They were published at 12 noon, in the office of the Utkal University. The university was then housed at the Vardaman compound in front of Ravenshaw College. I immediately left for the university on my cycle. On the way there, my friend Sourindra informed me that I had passed in the second division. But I wanted to see the result for myself. At the university campus, there was a huge crowd and it took me some time to see the blackboard where the result sheet had been affixed. I found that only four students from our school had passed in first division. Disappointed, I returned home. It then took about a week to obtain the marksheet from school. On receiving the marksheet, I found that my marks in optional mathematics were quite low. Besides, in the English second paper, my favourite subject, I had scored only 42, and that was the main reason I missed the first division. But I was quite sure that I would get admission into Ravenshaw College, and therefore, I obtained an application form and applied there.

Dr B. Samanta Rai, professor of botany in Ravenshaw College, was in charge of the intermediate (as +2 was known in those days, equivalent to 11th and 12th std.) admissions for that year. He was a friend of my uncle Braja Behari and knew my father very well. I, therefore, took the liberty of meeting him in his office once. Looking at my marksheet, he told me that I would get admission in first year science in the second list, but he could not assure whether I would get biology as fourth optional subject. He said that for the fourth optional subject, they would have an extra test, the marks of which would be added to the aggregate marks in the matriculation examination, based on which the seats would be allotted. The number of seats for biology as a fourth optional were limited, and since I intended studying medicine, I had to take biology as a subject. As an alternate plan, I thought that if I did not get biology as a fourth optional subject, I would leave mathematics and continue with physics, chemistry and biology. Though not necessary, the advantage of taking the fourth subject was that the marks obtained in the said subject minus the pass marks could be added to your aggregate. The first list of selected candidates for admission into intermediate was out in mid-June 1952. My name was not on that list. I became apprehensive and regretted having not applied for admission into Stewart Science College. While I was contemplating what I should do in case I did not get admission into Ravenshaw College, I got my letter of admission from the college, and was finally relieved and thanked God for his blessings. Thus began a new chapter in my life as a college student.

# College Life

Joining the first-year intermediate science class in Ravenshaw College, with physics, chemistry and mathematics as compulsory subjects and biology as the fourth optional subject, was considered an achievement for a student those days. Proud at having achieved this feat, I began making some preparations for the beginning of university life. What to wear to college was on top of my agenda. Though there was no fixed dress code, most of the students wore long pants and a half-sleeve shirt, and in winter, a pullover was worn over the shirt. As far as I remember, only one student out of about 135 students in class, Sharda Mohanty, who was from my school, wore half-pant and half-shirt to college, while another student, Niranjan Dwivedi, who later became a good friend of mine, wore a dhoti and shirt; he was from Ravenshaw Collegiate School. I was very particular about what I would wear and so had four full pants and four half-shirts stitched by a nearby tailoring shop. Since in the chemistry practical class the students would have to handle acids, I purchased a pair of sandals from the Bata shop in Chaudhary Bazaar. I also remember buying a couple of handkerchiefs, since the college benches were not cleaned regularly, so I would first place the handkerchief and then sit on it. I did this so that my clothes would not get dirty and could be worn at least for three days a week. I already had a bicycle and bought myself a lock so that nobody could steal it from the parking shed in college.

I remember, our classes started on 14th or 15th of July, my first lecture being chemistry. P. Brahma was the lecturer. My roll number was 119, and the experience of my first day in college is still fresh in my mind even 70 years later. There was a clamour among the students to occupy the front benches. In a class of 135 students, there were only seven girls. The very first row used to be kept for the girls, but usually they would take their seats only after the lecturer entered the classroom. Instead of trying to grab a seat in the front bench, I preferred to occupy a seat at the back, and hence entered through the back door. Incidentally, others who entered from the back door along with me were Ramesh Rath, whose father was the then education minister; Bijoy Pal, whose father was an eminent advocate of Orissa; Niranjan Dwivedi, whose brother was the famous socialist leader S.N. Dwivedi; and Ramesh Acharya, whose father had a medicine shop in Naya Sarak, Cuttack. We preferred to occupy the back benches so as to avoid questions from the lecturers and continued to occupy the same seat daily. Kulachandra Mishra, who had stood 4th in the university, too, became one of my most intimate friends and has remained so even today. Another friend, who was very shy but always very well-dressed, was Deva Priya Mohapatra, who had passed his Senior Cambridge from Madras, and his father was a judge in Orissa High Court. He became a close friend of mine not only in college but even later in life. We both followed the legal profession, and he finally became a judge in the Supreme Court serving at the same time as I served there. Deva died recently.

As I had taken biology as my fourth optional, we used to have classes starting at 9 am, and for those days, I used to get lunch money from my father. The usual place was the nearby Madras Café, which was the favourite eatery for us college students.

Our professors were highly reputed and quite well-known in their respective fields, and I remember them well even today. Dr Golakh Banerjee, the principal, was in the physics department; Dr B. Prasad was in the chemistry department; Dr B. Samanta Rai was the head of the department of botany; Dr Mukherjee was head of department of zoology; Dr Ramanath Mohanty was head of department of mathematics. English and Odia were compulsory subjects; and Professor B. Das, Dr O'Brien and Trilochan Mishra used to take our class in English. English was one of my favourite subjects, and Trilochan Mishra was a brilliant teacher. I cannot forget his impactful explanation of the poem/ballad "Inchcape Rock" written by the English poet Robert Southey. It was a fast-paced zesty poem about a warning bell on a reef at sea destroyed by a pirate so that he could plunder the ships that crashed into the reefs. In order to bring in the thrill and keep up the tempo, Trilochan sir gave an animated impression of a horse galloping towards us and then hitting the rock and collapsing. This incident is fresh in my mind even today. None of these professors are alive today, but their method of teaching and their interest in the students have left an indelible mark on me. The practical classes in science were taken by younger lecturers, though the senior lecturers always kept an eye. Dr Samanta Rai, especially, would often visit the laboratory and interact with us. A very humorous thing once happened when Dr Samanta Rai barged into our class and asked a student, sitting by my side, to draw a circle. When he did, Dr Samanta Rai gave him zero out of 25,000. He then drew a circle himself and asked that student to evaluate it wherein the student gave him zero out of 10 in return. Though a strict disciplinarian, he was amused and took it very lightly. Dr Samanta Rai was also very particular about the cleanliness of the entire college campus. Sometimes, we gathered near the chemistry lecture hall before time and ate groundnuts, making the floor dirty with the shells. If Dr Samanta Rai happened to pass by, he would insist that the students clean up the mess immediately.

The college quadrangle with a sundial in the middle used to have a grand appearance, with flower beds and a lush green grass lawn on all the four sections, starting from the portico-side entry to the Kanika Library at the other end. Most students would never take any other path than the path meant for walking and would never litter either the quadrangle or the lawn in any manner.

The Kanika Library, the oldest and biggest library in the state of Orissa, was housed in Ravenshaw College and was named after the Maharaja of Kanika, Rajendra Narayan Bhanjadeo, who had donated a large sum of money for its construction. The library, spread over 9,000 sq. ft, had an excellent collection of rare books. Though not exactly a bookworm, the books naturally warmed up to me. I enjoyed rummaging through the shelves. The feel of new books with their fresh crisp pages enticed me, while the smell of old books transported me back in time. Once a friend told me that the damp, musty smell that filled the Kanika Library was due to the fact that in a corner of the library the old volumes of many rare books and journals collected over decades had been bundled up in gunny bags, as they were too brittle to be held by hand.

The college portico used to be the hub for those who were active in sports. My cousin Umesh, who was in BA 3rd year then, was the football team captain and a popular figure not only among students but also with the professors. On the first day of college, after attending the first two classes, I headed to the college portico during the break, where I met my cousin who introduced me to some football players. They were quite friendly, and I soon got talking with them. When the break got over, I stood up to head for my next class, which was mathematics, the classroom room being quite close to the portico. It was then my cousin dissuaded me from attending the class by inviting me to have tea in a nearby shop with him and some of his teammates. As mathematics was not my favourite subject, his request became a temptation for me not to attend the class even though it was the very first class on the subject.

Life in college was totally different from life at school. There was no control imposed on us, neither by the professors nor at home from my father. It was a new kind of independence, and lecturers did not bother whether a student attended class or not. The only downside being that if a student got less than 65 per cent attendance, he would have to produce a medical certificate to be eligible to appear at the exam. The mad rush from one lecture hall to another was a thing to be seen. There used to be tutorial classes of smaller groups of students in subjects like mathematics and Odia. As I had no liking for mathematics, I neglected the subject totally but was conscious to make sure attendance did not fall short of 65 per cent.

During college days, my daily routine included an evening gathering of friends, *khatti*, for an hour to catch up on chit-chat on the riverbank. We would normally discuss the events of the day in class and outside besides catching up on all the gossip of the town that day. Visiting the cinema was also something I enjoyed immensely, especially since I had never visited a cinema hall during my entire school life of eight years, except for that one time with my uncle Braja Behari to watch the English movie *Great Expectations*. I think the fact that my father was a strict disciplinarian who imposed restrictive rules during my school life made me forget my essential duties of studying in order to build the foundation of a better future and successful career. Thus, in college, I was more drawn towards extracurricular activities like football, cricket, watching movies and, above all, the so-called friend's meeting on the riverbank. This freedom turned out to be disastrous for me in the long run. The high of being in college overshadowed my academic efforts. Time passed quickly and in mid-December we had our first semester examinations.

Just after the exams, five of us decided to embark on a bicycle trip to the famous Konark temple and Puri; the five included Ramesh Rath, Bijoy Pal, Kula Mishra, Ramesh Acharya and me. The contribution for the trip was Rs 20 per head.

Konark those days was not this big a tourist destination that it has now become. Situated on the coastline, the magnificent thirteenth-century temple was built by King Narasimhadeva I of the Ganga dynasty. Dedicated to the Sun God, Surya, it is an imposing 100-foot structure, intricately carved in stone. In the shape of a massive chariot with huge wheels and horses, it was often referred to as the 'Black Pagoda' by early European sailors. Though most of it has been destroyed over the centuries, it still stands in all its grandeur.

Since none of us had visited Konark before, we were awestruck to see the intricate carvings and sculptures. The 24 carved stone wheels with its eight spokes seemed to be pulling the chariot out of the sea when seen from land. These wheels also acted as sundials. Though many parts were in ruins, just seeing this magnificent work of architecture got us thinking about the capabilities of our forefathers. After taking a round of the structure, we started climbing to the top of the temple. In those days, there was absolutely no restrictions on accessing the temple. We could enter anywhere we liked, but there was no defined path and one had to be very careful while climbing, as there was no railing to hold on to. We used one of the idols for support to climb up to the next level. Much before sunset, all five of us reached the top of the temple where we sat waiting for the setting sun, discussing the history of our great state of Orissa, Kalinga architecture and how 1,200 sculptors had been engaged for the construction of the temple. Though Konark has changed, the temple still stands tall. The path we had taken years ago is no longer there today. However, over the years, whenever I visit Konark, I am reminded of our first visit to the temple premises in December 1952. It has a special place in my memory.

The next day, we proceeded to Puri. We had planned to go to the seashore and visit the Jagannath temple. Lord Jagannath is a form of Lord Vishnu, and the temple is considered one of the 'Char Dhams' or holy pilgrimage destinations every Hindu must visit in their lifetime. The temple was built in the twelfth century by King Anantavarman Chodaganga and completed by subsequent kings of the Ganga dynasty. The three main deities that reside here are Lord Jagannath, his brother Balabhadra and sister Subhadra. The statues of these three deities are carved out of neem wood and replaced every 12 years. We entered the temple at twilight. There was no electricity in the temple then, but the light from the lamps was enough for the worshipper to see and find their way in the temple. There are many smaller temples surrounding the main temple of Lord Jagannath, but we only visited the Vinayak and Lakshmi temples and finally the main temple. The three bejewelled deities looked radiant, and their jewels sparkled in the light of the lamps. After darshan, we rushed to the sea shore, which was down the road. The beach was overcrowded with tourists, particularly from Bengal and Bihar. We sat a while on the sand in front of the famous Puri Hotel, dipped our legs in the sea and splashed water at each other too.

This was one of my most enjoyable and memorable trips I have ever taken with friends, and I will always cherish the memories we made there. Of these five friends of mine, three have left this world, and only my friend Kula Mishra and I are still alive.

Few days after our trip to Konark, college reopened and the results of the first semester examination were declared. I was nervous as I had not done well in the examination, particularly in mathematics. The marks secured in physics, chemistry and biology were good, but in mathematics, very low. I resolved to work hard, so I decided I would stop visiting the riverbank every evening to see my friends and devote more time to my studies. I did so for a couple of days but could not resist the temptation of seeing my friends for long. I soon went back to my old habits, shamelessly ignoring my bad grades.

The second semester lasted from January to April, with the final examination in the last week of April. Lecturers did their job seriously but often rushed through the syllabus so as to complete the curriculum before the annual examination. I was finding it difficult to cope with the pressure. When the results of the final examination was declared, I had managed to secure reasonable marks in all papers except mathematics. I was promoted to the next year but had to drop mathematics. In other words, biology, which was my fourth optional subject, now became the third subject along with physics and chemistry. When I told my father about my grades, he simply said, 'Devote more time for studies.'

My mathematics grades coupled with my lack of interest in the subject should have made me realise that I was not meant for the Science stream. But my childhood dream of being a doctor and serving my village was so deep-rooted that I continued with science in the second year too. I resolved that I would devote my entire summer vacation to revising the first-year course. Though my intentions were good, I, unfortunately, fell ill during the break and spent the entire vacation in bed.

Second year classes started in earnest. Students became more serious about their studies. Except for the college election there was not much distraction. This time, even though I realised the pitfalls of my college way of life, there was no drastic change in my attitude and habits. Though

I had become a bit serious about my work and devoted more time to studies, my evening visits to the riverbank continued.

The final university examination was held in April, and the results came out in June. When I received my marksheet, I realised that I would not be able to secure admission into an Honours course, neither in botany nor zoology. I could have changed to the Arts stream then, like some of my friends did, but again I did not. My desire to join medical college was still strong, and I thought it would be easier to get into a medical college after a BSc degree. In Orissa, admission to medical college was done on the basis of the result in intermediate or BSc level. The selection procedure was first preference to BSc (Honours) then intermediate with first division, then BSc (Pass) and then intermediate with second division. So, I thought a BSc degree would assure admission into one of the medical colleges.

I knew that Ewing Christian College under Allahabad University had a good reputation and excellent teaching staff. I thought of applying there and told my father of my intention. My father readily agreed, even though it would be a strain on his finances. It meant an increased expense of Rs 125 per month besides other incidental expenses. With his consent, I hurriedly applied to Allahabad University. With my intermediate results having been declared in June and the Allahabad University classes to begin in the first week of July, I had no time to waste. So, without getting any intimation or admission confirmation from the college, I prepared to leave for Allahabad. Professor R.C. Lacy was the head of the department in botany there, and he was known to Dr Samanta Rai. As Dr Samanta Rai knew my father well, I got a letter from him for Professor Lacy and started my journey from Cuttack to Allahabad via Calcutta, where I was meeting my friend Bijoy for a day.

After meeting my friend in Kolkata, I caught the Bombay Mail to reach Allahabad. Since I had not received any intimation regarding my admission, I put my luggage in a hotel and, after taking a bath, left for the college office. On my way there, I met Prof. Lacy at his residence and gave him the letter of introduction from Dr Samanta Rai, and then proceeded to the college.

The hall where the admission process was underway was overcrowded, and I was probably the only one who was present without an intimation letter from the college, thus justifiably quite anxious. Seeing Prof. Lacy at the helm of affairs, I was a bit relieved and waited for my name to be called. After about ten people, my name was called out. Prof. Lacy asked me to go to the office to deposit the necessary fees. In a couple of days, I was also allotted my hostel room, room no. 4, in the RHEA hostel. Every room was meant for two students, and my roommate was Rishi Raj Khanna. He, however, was in another Science stream, namely physics, chemistry and mathematics, while I had taken up botany, zoology and chemistry.

The moment I arrived outside the hostel and took my luggage out of the rickshaw, I was surrounded by 2–3 persons who claimed to provide food to the hostellers. I signed up for a mess that provided non-vegetarian food. The hostel room was quite spacious; it had two beds and two study tables. From the window in the room, we could see the main college building. Every block had an attendant that cleaned the rooms twice a day and also made the bed. There were common shower and toilet facilities for students on the ground floor of the building. There was a canteen outside the college campus, where I used to have snacks and tea in the afternoon. A man selling cakes and pastries also visited our hostel. I opened an account in every eating place, and the payment for meals consumed was made at the end of every month. My father was very particular, and I used to receive Rs 125 through insured cover on the first of every month.

After about 15 days of the college reopening, the usual ragging began. I had heard about the same but had never experienced it. The experience was quite novel and at the same time a bit unnerving. Around 10–11 pm at night the senior students would gather together and call the newcomers one by one, commanding them to do various odd jobs, asking several embarrassing questions and at times subjecting them to physical ordeal. Luckily for me, there was no physical torture. But I was grilled for more than an hour and had to tolerate various slangs from different seniors. Though I had heard that ragging went on for several days, that was all there was to that night's ordeal. I do not know what purpose it serves but I will admit that when I was in my final year of BSc, I also meted out the same treatment to newcomers in the hostel.

The college was located on the banks of the Yamuna River. It was one of the oldest colleges in Allahabad, managed by a Christian mission in the USA. Thus, one gentleman from the USA would always be present as teaching staff in the college campus. During my time, the gentleman was Mr Brubecker. Since it was a Christian missionary institution, a good number of students belonging to the Christian community from different parts of the country studied there. We had students from Kerala, Madhya Pradesh and Rajasthan. A sizable number of students from Orissa, particularly from districts of Kalahandi and Balangir, were also studying in the college.

After a few days of settling in, our classes started in full swing. There were a couple of girls in our class, but there were a greater number of girls in the intermediate classes. There used to be a general knowledge competition between the intermediate students and the graduate class students in the college common hall known as Toker Hall. The principal,

Mr S.S. Gideon, used to conduct it himself. The graduate classes won in both the years, and I was declared the champion on both occasions.

The college also had a student union for which an election was held annually, but I never had any interest to be an office bearer so never ran for any post. I did, however, serve as a college prefect and as chief prefect in my final year, a highly respected position among students. As a college prefect, I once had an altercation with a local goon, who passed some comments during a congregation. Later he also threatened me. But I made it clear to him that if he harmed me or did anything untoward inside the college campus then I would complain to the police. This threat worked like magic.

Even in Allahabad, I continued to devote considerable time to extracurricular activities, though not at the cost of my studies. Besides other sports, as a member of the boat club, we used to hire a boat and go sailing on the Yamuna, especially on moonlit nights.

Visits to Civil Lines in Allahabad, a very popular destination on weekend evenings, was a regular feature. Spending a couple of hours in India Coffee House over a cup of coffee and a plate of cashew nuts was a common pastime. Cinemas used to be very cheap, particularly the night shows. I once had an embarrassing experience returning after a late-night movie show. As I was coming to my room, suddenly the hostel warden appeared and confronted me for returning so late, to which I politely replied that I had gone for a night show. He was not amused and angrily threatened to write to my father. I then told him quite arrogantly, 'Sir, my father has sent me here alone so far away from home, only because he has full trust in me. So, you can go ahead and write to him.' Having said that, I came back to my room, but I spent the next 15 days, expecting a letter of chastisement from my father. I did not receive the letter; it seems the warden's threat was an empty one.

In college, I developed friendships with several people, the closest among them were Harish Aggarwal and Satish Oberoi, who were both day scholars. Among the boarders, my friends were Vijay Seth, K.D. Joshi, Baikunth Nath, and few others. During that time, although I lost touch with most of my Ravenshaw College friends, I was in close touch with Bijoy, who was graduating in Calcutta. My friend Kula Mishra had once come and stayed with me in the hostel for two days, and I, too, had stayed with him at IIT Kharagpur for one night on my way to Allahabad. I also regularly corresponded with my school friend Sovan, who was pursuing his studies in Delhi.

Life in college was quite enjoyable. My friendly demeanour made me a popular figure in the hostel, and my extracurricular activities made me a well-known student in college, both among the students and the staff.

While in Allahabad, in the month of November, the Industries Fair was being held in Pragati Maidan, Delhi, and our college organised an excursion to Delhi. I was also in the group of about 30, including five or six girls from the intermediate section, selected for the trip to Delhi. In Delhi we stayed at the Modern School hostel, as the school was closed for a vacation. We visited the Industries Fair for two consecutive days. Though there was a mad rush at the exhibition, it was very interesting, as there I saw a television for the first time.

As it was my first visit to Delhi, we visited several historical monuments like the Red Fort, Qutub Minar, Humayun's Tomb, etc. We visited a stadium where a parade and programme were conducted for students on the occasion of Prime Minister (PM) Jawaharlal Nehru's birthday, celebrated in the country as Children's Day. Mr Nehru attended the function personally and spent time with the children, which was quite special for us. We also went to Connaught Place to join the fanfare in welcoming the Soviet PM Nikolai Bulganin and Communist Party secretary Nikita Khrushchev, who were in India for the first official visit of Soviet leaders after Independence.

After Delhi, we went on to Agra, staying there for two days. We visited the two most magnificent buildings there—the Agra Fort and the Taj Mahal. The grandeur and magnificence of these monuments were beyond what I had witnessed ever before in my life. This visit left a lasting impression on my mind that is still afresh. I must have visited the Taj and Agra Fort a number of times in the course of my life, but the charm of the first visit as a student in Allahabad was quite different and distinct.

I still remember how during my time in Allahabad, Mrs Indira Gandhi visited our campus and addressed the students on one occasion. What a moment of pride it was for me as chief prefect, involved with arrangements and maintaining student discipline. Another time, singer Talat Mohammad came to our institution and sang to a jam-packed hall for about 30 minutes.

Another incident during my university days that had a lasting impact on me was the occasion of Diwali. Most of the students in the hostel played *teen-patti* (a type of card game) on Diwali night. I was also invited to join a few friends for a game of card. Although reluctant, my friends were persuasive, and I decided to play with Rs 25 only. The game continued till 2 am, and by the end of it, I had lost about Rs 75. I couldn't sleep the rest of the night thinking of how I would manage my expenses for the rest of the month. I did not pay my mess and restaurant bills, asking for time till I received money from home. I then wrote to my father telling him that, given the extreme winter conditions in Allahabad, I needed to buy two jackets for which I needed an extra Rs 200. In December, I received the extra amount with which I purchased one jacket and used the balance amount to pay up my dues. Since that day I have never played cards with monetary stakes.

Once while interacting with Mr Brew Baker, our hostel warden, I had indicated that I was desirous of joining the medical college after graduation, but could not do so after my intermediate, as I did not have the necessary marks. He immediately offered me admission to Christian Medical College, Vellore, on the condition that I convert to Christianity, as the missionaries had some reserved seats at that college only for Christian students. Christian Medical College, Vellore, had a good reputation at the national level, and I was, therefore, tempted initially to accept the offer. However, on second thought, I thought it was immoral to change my faith for this. That apart, for a science graduate, admission to a medical college in Orissa was a certainty back then.

So, with a degree in Science from Allahabad University I was back in Cuttack and planned to join the medical college at Cuttack. Before applying, I went to meet a friend who had studied with me in Ravenshaw College. He had joined the medical college after his intermediate, and I thought it wise to discuss my plans with him. There, the sheer sight of voluminous medical books in his hostel room made me realise that a five-year medical course was not my cup of tea. I decided not to join the medical college and gave up my childhood dream of becoming a doctor.

Around that time, my father had just about one year of service before superannuation. My younger brother was pursuing his BSc degree in Ravenshaw College. My younger sister was still unmarried. I realised my father still had many unfinished responsibilities. Like every father looking for some financial assistance from the eldest son, particularly when his worldly liabilities were not over, my father, too, wanted me to join the Orissa secretariat as an assistant, where one could expect to retire as a deputy secretary. He suggested that I simultaneously appear for some competitive examinations at either the state or national level. Though my father had made a career in the Orissa secretariat, I had no such inclination and was looking for an alternative avenue.

My maternal uncle, who was commissioner of Income Tax in Calcutta, had come to visit during those days and was staying with us. I requested him to get me a job in a multinational company. He advised me to get a law degree after which he could easily push me into a company job. With that intention in mind, I joined Madhusudan Law College in Cuttack.

Madhusudan Law College, or MS Law College, had no building of its own and the classes were being held in Ravenshaw College. Classes were scheduled from 7–9:30 am. Very often, out of three classes a day, I was not able to attend the first class, but my attendance was being marked by proxy. Though I liked the subject, I studied law with the least seriousness. Life in law college was more casual in the sense that most of the students had taken up law only as a stop-gap arrangement. There were only a few serious students. The course was not very intense, and I found time for extracurricular activities. My closest friends in law college were D.M. Patnaik, L.N. Patnaik and G.C. Jena.

In MS Law College, Mr Murti, who was the principal, was the only full-time professor and all others were part-time professors, such as Dr B.N. Mishra, B.K. Roy, M.N. Das, S.N. Acharya and S.C. Roy. Of them, S.N. Acharya, B.K Roy and B.N. Mishra ended their career as judges of the high court, and S.C. Roy as the advocate general for the state.

When lectures ended, my friends and I spent an hour playing table tennis. I used to get back home by 11 am, and after lunch, nap for an hour.

I would then head out for the tennis ground for a good game of tennis. Our tennis court was within the railway campus in front of Ravenshaw College. Our college professors S.N. Acharya and B.N. Mishra used to join us sometimes. After the game, we visited the nearby Gujarati restaurant for snacks. Most evenings I would spend time with my friends in their hostel rooms. D.M. Patnaik was a good singer and used to entertain us by singing and playing the harmonium. By the time I reached home, it would be around 8:30 or 9 pm.

Law college made me a sportsman. I represented the college as part of the cricket team in the inter-college competition. D.M. Patnaik and I even became college champion in doubles, both in tennis and table tennis.

My father retired while I was still at law college. He had a meagre pension of Rs 500 per month. I knew that resources were scarce, so one evening, when G.N. Mitra, who was then the director of the fisheries department, had come to our house and offered me a job for the post of an inspector in his directorate, I was very keen. This would fetch me a salary of about Rs 270 per month plus the dearness allowance. The pay scale was almost similar to that of a college lecturer or a deputy collector in the administrative service. I was interested and asked him about the prospect of promotion in the organisation. He replied that if one did well, I could retire as director like him. I agreed to join the job but wanted to be permitted to continue with my law classes. This, he frankly refused, and so I continued with my law course while simultaneously preparing for the civil services exams. Infact, I did appear for one exam with history, botany and law as my subjects. I, however, did not get any interview call, and when my marksheet from UPSC reached me, I figured out why. My marks in the law paper was miserable. I was toying with the idea of taking another chance, but it remained in the realm of my mind.

An interesting incident worth mentioning transpired during my second year as a law student. Dr S.K. Ghosh was teaching us the Indian Constitution. On the topic of dealing with the appointment and removal of judges of the high courts, he stated that a judge can be removed by process of impeachment by the state legislature whereas a judge of the Supreme Court can be impeached by the Parliament only. I immediately raised my hand to voice my doubt. When questioned, I said that possibly he was wrong, since the state legislature has no role to play and it is only in Parliament where an impeachment proceeding can be initiated and taken. He, however, insisted on being correct and decided to place a bet with me. I was pretty sure, so I accepted his challenge and held out a Rs 10 note. He took the money and left only to return a little later, smiling. He declared he was wrong and gave me Rs 20 in return. Needless to say, after class that day, our snacks party at the Gujarati restaurant was a grand one. Dr Ghosh had earned a doctorate in law from an American university, and comparative constitution was his special paper. I realised how sometimes a wrong notion can get embedded in one's mind, but I was impressed that he was magnanimous enough to accept his mistake.

Even though I was not that serious in law classes, I never missed a single moot court class and participated in each and every one the college organised. I became the champion in my class and also in the combined moot court, for which I won the Running Trophy and Rs 200 as the prize.

After passing the law degree, I anxiously awaited communication from my uncle in Calcutta who had assured me of a job in a private company. My father had retired from his service and was managing the household with his meagre pension. I felt rather guilty, as my father had spent a good amount on my studies in Allahabad with the hope of me studying medicine. Luckily, the wait did not last long and I soon received a letter of appointment as a sales representative of Burmah Shell in Calcutta, with a monthly salary of Rs 800 and a company car.

The thought of getting a hefty salary and perks attached to the job made me dance with joy. In those days, a Class II officer in the Orissa government, whether a deputy collector or a lecturer or an engineer, used to be absorbed in the scale of Rs 200–700. Even the salary of an IAS officer at the entry level was about Rs 450 per month. My father was overjoyed. My close friends even started making plans of spending the Durga Puja vacation with me in Calcutta.

At that juncture, I met a well-wisher of mine, whose opinion I held in high regard. When I went to his house one evening and told him about the job, he conveyed his blessing and best wishes. But at the end, he told me to think over my decision carefully. He pointed out how I wanted to make a difference in society and whether this job would provide me the satisfaction of doing so. His words struck a chord with me and I spent the night in deep thought. I realised he was correct and decided against accepting the job. At that point of time, I had no other offer in my hand, and thought I had no option left other than joining the legal profession. Knowing fully well the uncertainty in the legal profession, I decided to take the risk. When I broke this news to my father the next morning, he was furious and didn't speak to me. When I conveyed my decision to my maternal uncle in Calcutta who had arranged for this job, he, too, was disappointed. Most of my family members did not take my decision of joining the legal profession well. It was only my mother who wholeheartedly supported me and encouraged me to choose a career that would bring me satisfaction as a professional. I, therefore, jumped into the legal profession with the resolve that either I would survive as a successful lawyer or I would perish trying. I decided to put all my efforts into making a name for myself as a good lawyer and a place for myself in the legal profession.

One important thing that I would like to mention here is that there should always be open and cordial communication between a father and a son. Those days, fathers were the providers for the family and commanded respect. Every word spoken by him was considered an order never to be broken. Since women/mothers stayed at home to look after the children, the bond she shared with them was closer. Whether it was for the benefit of one's ego or to avoid clashes, sons spoke very little to their fathers and were always close to their mothers. This, though, I feel is not very productive. In certain aspects, like education and career choices, mutual consultation between father and children is always fruitful. With age, comes experience and maturity, and it would be advantageous for a father to share his views with his children and respect their opinions too.

From my childhood, I was so afraid of my father, and throughout my life, I never challenged what he said nor seek any serious advice from him. Even when I lived with him alone in Cuttack, as my mother was away in my village, I never dared to question him. My father took care of everything, and I had no freedom to even suggest anything to him. In school, I put all my efforts into getting better grades in the class purely out of my fear of being reprimanded by my father. This relationship was obviously not a congenial one. Consequently, when I tasted the freedom during college life, I misused it, neglecting my studies and enjoying a totally carefree life at that young age of 15 or 16.

On the other hand, as a father myself I have ensured to maintain an open and cordial relationship with my children. Right from the time they were born, I have tried to be a part of their lives. I have never interfered with the choices, but at the same time, made it a point to engage them in conversations. Being a well-established lawyer and subsequently a judge, I would have liked one of my children to become a lawyer, though I have never imposed that thought on them. In fact, later, my second son, who has an MBA and also a law degree, decided to become a lawyer after working in the corporate sector for around 10 years. At that point of time, I was a judge of the Supreme Court and had a fair understanding of life, especially that of a lawyer, and struggles in a big city like Delhi. I genuinely encouraged him to continue in the profession but only advised him that it would be convenient for him to start practising in Orissa High Court, since life in Delhi would be much more competitive and harder. However, I also told him that if he wanted to continue as a lawyer in Delhi, he should have an establishment of his own and should not reside with me in my official quarters, as I thought it unethical in my profession. He, however, chose to go back to the corporate sector and joined a company in Delhi. This is interpreted by many as a discouragement to my son, with which I do not agree at all. I would have been the happiest father if one of my children became a lawyer.

# My Legal Journey, How it all Began

In those days, a person wanting to practise law had two options—he could either enrol as a pleader and start practising in the lower courts and then enrol himself as an advocate after completing three years or he could undergo training for one year as an article clerk in the office of a senior advocate and thereafter start practising in the high court.

After much consideration, I decided to join the office of Bimal Krishan Pal, a senior advocate and the father of my friend Bijoy Pal, who was studying in the medical college in Cuttack. The next morning, I got ready and went straight to the residence of Mr Pal. I shared my predicament and also explained my decision despite the financial condition of my family. After a 20-minute discussion, he said I could join his office that very evening.

I still remember that first day vividly. I reached the office of Mr Pal, but the door was closed. Mr Pal, however, had seen me from the upper balcony of his double-storey residence and asked me to open the office and wait inside. As I opened the door, the smell of incense wafting through the air reached me. There was a big study table with an armchair on one side, obviously meant for my senior, and three chairs in front of the desk, probably meant for the juniors. There was also a wooden bench in the room, and that is where I took a seat. Mr Pal came down to the office wearing a dhoti, kurta and a long pair of socks, holding his spectacles in his hand. The first thing he told me was to not sit on the bench, as it was meant for the clients. Mr Pal then went about preparing for the evening, settling in the armchair and putting on his specs while speaking to me. He gave me an insight into the legal profession and emphasised that the profession though lucrative in the long run also meant hard work and sincerity. One piece of advice he shared was to never waste time gossiping in the Bar Association. He also emphasised that even if one didn't have any work, one should spend time in the courtroom observing how cases are conducted, what is required and what amount of preparedness a judge expects from a lawyer.

At this juncture, his clerk Bacha Babu reached the office. Mr Pal introduced him to me and called for a file where one of the parties had died. Handing over that file to me, he asked me to draft a petition for substitution. He then asked me under which provision a petition was to be filed, and even though I replied correctly that it was order 22 of the Civil Procedure Code, he still asked me to refer to the provision from the book before writing the petition. According to him, nothing should be done without looking at the book, however well-versed one may be with the provision of law.

While I was reading the relevant provision of law relating to substitution, my friend Deva reached and took the chair by my side. He had already been enrolled as an advocate and had started practising by then. Mr Pal discussed some cases with him, which were to be heard the next day, and asked him to prepare for some of the cases in a particular direction. At that point of time, Mahima Shankar Rai, a very senior lawyer, who used to be a junior in Mr Pal's office, arrived. Though he now appeared for cases independently, he at times attended the office of Mr Pal. Mr Pal discussed some old cases with him and then started reading some files, possibly a case which he would argue the next day. At around 8 pm, three cups of tea for juniors and a cup of Horlicks for Mr Pal arrived.

After about an hour, he enquired whether I had completed the application. When I handed him the application I had drafted, he went through the same minutely and made several corrections. He asked me to rewrite it, address the corrections and incorporate his suggestions. I rewrote the entire document and showed it to him for the second time, but he was still not satisfied and asked me to write it again. By that time, my friend Deva had left and so had Mr Rai. The clerk, too, had left the office at 10 pm. Just then, Mr Pal's domestic help came in from the house and announced that the dinner was ready, to which Mr Pal replied that he would come after 15 minutes. He then looked up at me and asked me whether my draft was complete. He said he would only leave after finalizing my draft. Within 5 minutes, I showed him another draft, and this time Mr Pal was finally satisfied. He said the legal profession was about looking at the books, assimilating the same and expressing either in writing while drafting or addressing the court orally. According to him, one could only master this with practice. After this, he said I could go back home. As I was leaving his office, he instructed me to reach the high court by 10:30 am the next day.

It was 10:30 pm by the time I left on my bicycle, and all the roads were deserted and the shops had closed. I thought to myself that I did not join the medical college being afraid of voluminous books, thus thwarting my dream of becoming a doctor, but the profession I had ultimately chosen would require a lifetime of reading voluminous books and files. But there was no looking back. I resolved to work hard to establish myself as a good lawyer. When I reached home, everybody had gone to sleep except my mother, who was waiting for me so that we could have dinner together. She then brought food for us and sat down to discuss my first day, telling me that if I worked sincerely, I could certainly make a name for myself. That was her wish and blessing for me. Even today, I can feel her love every time I remember those few words she had said. Her encouragement was heartwarming since not only the members of our family but even people known to us did not appreciate my decision of choosing the legal profession. In those days, generally people were not attracted towards the legal profession, especially first-generation lawyers. It was only people who had lawyers in the family who joined the profession so that it would be easier for them professionally and financially, since neither there was any need for investment in a library nor the worry of how to attract clients. In fact, I had just one other distant relative who had retired as an additional district magistrate and would tell me that the legal profession was the best profession where one could prosper.

Office in the morning, high court from 10:30 am to 4:30 pm, back to office in the evening—this was my routine for a period of one year. My friend Deva and I used to travel together. Even though he used his father's car on other occasions, he never came to court by car. That one year of training was a tough time for me, as I was an adult and did not feel like asking my father, who had also retired from service by then, for money. Occasionally, Mr Pal used to pay me something small, even though legally I was not entitled to earn. So those payments were almost like a gift from God for me. It was Mr Pal, my senior's method of teaching, his encouragement and consoling words that were my real earnings.

One year passed very quickly, and by September 1961, I was entitled to be enrolled as an advocate in the high court. The fee for enrolment was Rs 1,800 besides the cost of procuring a black coat, a gown and few bands. The total would cost about Rs 2,500. I had told my father about the same, but as he was still angry with me for turning down the job offer from Burmah Shell in favour of becoming a lawyer, so he flatly denied. I had to wait till February 1962 when the Bar Council Act came into force and the control over the lawyers was transferred from the high court to the Bar Council of Orissa. The new enrolment fee was only Rs 250. Between September 1961 and Jan 1962, I had earned some money in Mr Pal's office, which was enough for me to acquire the required dress and gown and also to pay the enrolment fee. I was finally enrolled as an advocate in February 1962, part of the first batch of lawyers to be enrolled under the Bar Council Act. My *sanad* (licence) was signed by the Late B. Mahapatra, who was the president of the Bar Council, and R.N. Mishra, who was the secretary. R.N Mishra later went on became a judge and ultimately retired as the Chief Justice of India (CJI). From 1 March 1962, began a new chapter in my life as an advocate in Orissa High Court. Along with me, two batchmates of mine from law college, Bijan Roy and Mrs A.K. Padhi, were also enrolled, and Mrs Padhi became a colleague of mine on the bench.

I have often pondered over my father's reaction and refusal to give me the necessary money to enrol myself as advocate. In retrospect, I realise that had I been in my father's position, I would have probably acted in a similar manner. When my father retired, my younger brother was in his fourth year of college and my younger sister was still unmarried. Like many fathers, on retirement, my father, too, looked forward to some financial support from his eldest son, especially since his liabilities were not over yet. Naturally, therefore, any parent would have been angry, and my father was no exception. The initial years as a lawyer were full of struggles, and therefore, till about 1970, my father was hopeful that I would leave the legal profession and take up a well-paying job. Later on, though, he was happy to see me do well, particularly when I became the government advocate, and senior officers from the Orissa secretariat would often come to me for necessary help pertaining to the cases of their department pending in Orissa High Court.

On the first day of my career as an advocate, I earned Rs 50 by signing the *vakalatnama* in two different cases that our clerk had kept ready, and that initial amount I kept as a memento for quite some time. The clerk then told me that I should go to the court of Justice G.K. Mishra where Mr Pal would be arguing in some matter. At that point in time, there were only four judges, including the chief justice, and the latest inclusion was Justice G.K. Mishra. His nephew was a friend of mine, and with him I had gone to his residence while I was studying law to invite him to various functions. During my articleship, too, I had interacted with him on several occasions. So out of the four judges, only one judge knew me. The other three judges, Justice S. Burman, Justice R.K. Das and Chief Justice R.L. Narashingham, did not even know my name, though I had appeared before them on some occasions when I argued cases on behalf of Mr Pal. It was only after Justice Das retired in 1967 that I visited his house for the first time with his son-in-law, who was also an advocate then. After that, every year I used to be a guest at his home on Dussehra Day for lunch. His grandson, Pradeep, went on to become a judge of Orissa High Court and was later on appointed as chief justice of Jharkhand High Court, and post retirement, he is now a member of the Lokpal. The object of this narration is to tell you that it doesn't matter if your name is not known to the judges for a couple of years when starting your career, unlike lawyers whose fathers were or are judges, who are congratulated by each judge when he or she appears for the very first time in court. What matters eventually is to earn a name as a successful lawyer with hard work, confidence, sincerity and honesty.

Justice G.K. Mishra was a very hard task master and would not spare even the senior-most member of the Bar if they were unprepared with the brief he handled. His harsh words were unpalatable, but his analysis of a matter and his ultimate judgement was undoubtedly of a very high order. I personally felt confident in his court, and Mr Pal used to entrust me with even difficult cases to argue before him. One evening, around a month after my enrolment, Mr Pal handed over a brief to me, it was a second appeal. He told me that I would have to argue the matter independently. l had never expected a big opportunity like this so soon in my career. Nervous yet excited at the prospect, I took the brief and after coming back home, made extensive handwritten notes (about 20 pages).

The next day, when the case was called, I stood up to argue. The court asked me to state the facts and the findings of the two courts below. I did that so efficiently that Justice Mishra appeared to be pleased. He then asked, on what point of law I was challenging the case, to which I stated something which was not acceptable to him. My entire argument stood concluded in about 15 minutes. The judgement was delivered, and it went against us. Justice Mishra, however, appreciated the manner in which I represented the case and indicated the same in the judgement itself. Mr Pal, who was sitting behind me, said nothing then, but when I reached his office in the evening, he told me that the result would have been the same had he argued the matter himself and praised me for my method of submission. He then handed me two second appeals for admission. Having argued one matter before Justice Mishra, I had gained much confidence, and the next day, both my second appeals were admitted by him. This gave me immense pleasure, since in those days, the court used to be very strict in admitting second appeals and usually would not admit it unless there was a substantial question of law involved. I was also paid a handsome amount for these two cases.

Few days thereafter a very strongly contested matter relating to riparian rights between sets of villagers of two villages was listed for hearing. The name of the village was Gandibed in the Balasore district near Nilgiri. Our party was the plaintiff, and they were the downstream landowners. The defendants were the villagers living upstream, who, taking advantage of their location, dug a canal and diverted water to their field at a distance of 3–5 km. As a consequence, the village downstream did not get any water. Both courts below had rejected our case on the ground that they (defendants) being upper riparian owners had the natural right of easement to get the water from the river, and the court had no power to issue order of injunction. Mr Pal himself read the brief for about half an hour and then handed over the file to me to argue the matter. I was really surprised as to how come that in such a contested matter, where the villagers had paid substantial fees, I was being asked to argue. I thought to myself that there was possibly a slim chance of getting a judgement in our favour and that is why the brief was given to me. Mr Pal handed me a Rs 100 note and told me this was a case on easementary right. I took the brief and the book on easement laws and went home. Having read and noted the findings of the courts below, I thought of only one solid question to use as my argument in court, namely: who can be said to be a riparian owner? Could a landowner having his land at a distance of 3 miles from the riverbank claim a riparian right of easement? One of the witnesses had said that his land was at a distance more than 3 miles.

When the case was called upon, my opponent, who was my teacher from school, stood up and said that there was concurrent finding of fact and as such no merit in this appeal. Justice Mishra got annoyed and told him he would have his turn. I was then asked to argue the brief. I very succinctly narrated the facts, along with the relief sought in prayer, and also indicated the findings arrived at on different issues involved. Then I urged only one question, namely who could be held to be a riparian owner to get an easementary right to take water from the river. I urged that certainly the owners of the land abutting the river or up to a reasonable distance could be held to be riparian owners but not villagers whose land was at a distance of more than 3 miles from the riverbed. When I formulated the question of law and stated it before the learned judge, he mulled over it for 2 minutes and appeared to have accepted my submission. He then asked the opposing lawyer to reply. The opposing lawyer only harped upon the latest judgement of the Supreme Court had enunciated a principle that a finding of fact arrived at by the appellate court could not be reversed by a high court in exercise of power of under section 100 of Civil Procedural Code, however gross or erroneous it may be. They were referring to the judgement of Justice K.C. Das Gupta of the Supreme Court. The learned judge told the counsel that what had been argued was not a challenge to the finding arrived at but a pure question of law relating to the very concept of riparian ownership. The counsel appearing for the respondent, on finding that the judge was not accepting his submission, asked for adjournment on the ground that senior counsel Mr Ranjit Mohanty would argue this case. Justice Mishra did grant the permission but mentioned that irrespective of who argued the case, Mr Mohanty or the attorney general, the outcome would be the same. He also asked me to look up similar case laws, particularly any decision of an American court.

When I reached Mr Pal's office that evening, he told me that the case was going on very well and asked the villagers, who were already present there, to pay the balance fees. They immediately gave Rs 2,000. Mr Pal gave me Rs 200 and told me that the argument I made was really satisfactory. As I had a day's gap before the next hearing, I devoted the entire day to reading in the high court library. I looked up Halsbury's *Law of England* and the American cases too. I suddenly noticed a case somewhat similar, though not identical in nature, so I took down the reference. In those days, there was no computer, and to get a reference was a difficult task, but having laboured for the whole day, I felt relieved when I found the reference in question.

The next day, since our case was a part-heard matter, it was put up as the first case on the list. I called for the reference from the library and was going through the same. Mr Ranjit Mohanty argued the matter for about two hours till the lunch interval. When the court broke for lunch, Justice Mishra asked me as to how much I received towards my fees. I was forced to reveal the amount, and then the judge asked me to ask Mr Pal to be present in the court. After lunch, Justice Mishra told Mr Pal that I was arguing the case very well and he should increase my fee to at least Rs 500. Having said so, he asked me to continue with my argument. I then read a passage from Halsbury's *Law of England* as to the meaning of a riparian owner and read the US judgement. He appreciated my research and told me that sincere labour was always rewarded. He then asked Mr Mohanty if he would like to say anything more, to which the answer was nothing further. When we came out, Mr Mohanty, a tall figure, embraced me and congratulated me by saying that my argument was outstanding. In the evening, the villagers again reached the office and before Mr Pal uttered anything, they themselves came out with another Rs 1,000 rupees, out of which he gave me another Rs 200. Thus, I could earn a sum of Rs 500, which was undoubtedly a handsome amount in those days. That day, I also thought to myself that I had made the right decision in life by taking up law as my career.

After about 10 days, the daily cause list of the high court showed that our appeal had been listed for delivery of judgement. I was nervous and anxious to know the result of my first contested argument. I distinctly remember that I was the first person to reach the court that day. My opposing counsel, including senior advocate Mr Ranjit Mohanty, was also present in court. As soon as court was in session, the judgement was declared and our second appeal had been allowed. Mr Mohanty, though my opposing counsel, gave me a hug and quietly congratulated me. I then got the copy of the judgement from the bench clerk and went through the same. I found that Justice Mishra had not only accepted all my contentions but had praised my argument at several places. When I came out of the courtroom, Mr Pal also thanked me profusely. I felt as though I had won a great battle. I have won several cases on very important matters thereafter, but that pleasure of winning my first big case has not been replicated.

Thereafter Mr Pal became so confident about my ability that he allowed me to argue several second appeals and civil revisions in the court of Justice G.K Mishra. The very opportunity to argue so many cases was a unique experience for me. In the initial stage, we were only two juniors in the office of Mr Pal—D.P. Mohapatra and myself. Later on, another friend from Puri, A. Mohanty, joined. About two years later, my friend and Mr Pal's son Bijoy, too, got enrolled as an advocate and joined the office. After Bijoy joined the office, he started managing the office, including the fees to be paid to the juniors. Even though he was a close friend of mine, I felt it was time for to me to move on.

I worked in the office of Mr B.K. Pal for five years, from 1962 to 1967. During those five years, if on any day I was absent from his office, he would visit me at my house with bread in his hand on the assumption that I was unwell. During summer, when we used to cycle to commute, his constant advice was to put on a hat so that the heat would not harm us. I was treated like a son. Since Mr Pal was an eminent civil lawyer and was considered as the most learned lawyer on tenancy law, I had the opportunity to build a solid foundation in civil and tenancy law, and thereafter on that foundation I built up my reputation in these two fields by my own perseverance and industry. It would not be an exaggeration if I said that my success in the legal profession was a result of my rich experience in the office of Mr Pal, and I believe it is his blessings which ultimately made it possible for me to reach the topmost position in law. I cannot forget the day when I was elevated as a judge of the high court and went to meet a bedridden Mr Pal that evening, he touched my head and said, 'You will go far in your career and rise to the top.' He gave me his blessings, with tears in his eyes.

As far as I remember, I used to earn about Rs 600–700 per month at Mr Pal's office. Those five years as a lawyer were quite enjoyable and I never faced any financial instability. Now that I was doing well, talk of my marriage kept coming up. In the early part of 1962, my friend Bijoy Pal got married. Another close friend, Kula Mishra, got married in 1963. The same year two other close friends, Ramesh Rath and D.P. Mahapatra, also got married. From the beginning of 1964, my mother started nagging me to get married. Our neighbour, a sales tax officer, whose daughter was a doctor, had sent the proposal of her marriage to me, but I had quietly told my mother I would not like to marry a doctor.

In the meanwhile, my father, who had been retired since 1960 and till then had not been able to purchase a piece of land to construct a residential house, finally purchased a piece of land in Reba Colony, Kafla. After purchasing the land, he said that it was the responsibility of the children to build the house. My younger brother was working as agricultural supervisor in the department of fruit preservation. We were thinking as to how to get started on the house, and it was decided that a sum of Rs 15000 would be taken as loan from the Housing Cooperative Bank by my father, and the annual instalment would be paid back by us two brothers. My engineer friend, Gopal Mitra, gave the drawing, which we got approved in the municipality office, and on getting the loan, the construction work began. It was an 1800 sq. ft house, with three bedrooms, a drawing room, a kitchen and a store and two bathrooms. Initially, the construction work went on with great speed, but when the loan amount got over, the work slowed down. We had to find a supplier who would supply bricks on loan. In those days, there was a scarcity of cement, but my father's friend, who was an officer in the supply department, helped us in procuring a wagonload of cement from a cement factory in Rajgangpur. The roof of the house was cast in January 1966. With the meagre income from my practice and my brother's contribution, we paid off the loan instalment and continued the house construction.

Just after the roof of our house was cast, my mother started insisting that I get married. Even though I used to tell her that the construction work would take at least another year or more to be completed and we had financial difficulties, she would not listen to me.

Sometime in the later part of 1966, while I was coming down from the courtroom to the Bar library, I met Barrister B.M. Patnaik who was also distantly related to me. He suddenly asked me whether I could join his office either in the morning or in the evening? I immediately answered in the affirmative, since by then I had decided to leave the office of Mr Pal. I was toying with the idea as to whether I should join some other senior's office or if I should start my own independent practice. My dilemma arose from the fact that I was not sure I would be able to get sufficient clients on my own, besides the house construction was only halfway through, and the annual repayment of loan was still going on. I feared that if I did not earn anything, then it would be a difficult situation for me. I decided, therefore, to postpone starting my independent practice and joined the office of Barrister B.M. Patnaik, preferring the morning shift.

Mr Patnaik was related to me; his wife and my mother were cousins, and he was very close to my father. On his return from England after becoming a barrister, he had stayed in a rented house near our house in Oriya Bazaar. His children, Ruby and Bulu, used to come and play with us every evening. However, by the time I joined his office, he had purchased a large house in Bhasakosh Lane, with a fairly extensive lawn in the front.

The next day, I called on Mr Patnaik around 7 am; I had already informed Mr Pal that I wouldn't be able to make it to his chamber in the morning. Mr Patnaik was sipping tea while reading the newspaper. While he was talking to me, a man arrived and told him that his son had been arrested under the Preventive Detention Act and he was required to submit a representation. Mr Patnaik collected the papers he had with him, which consisted of an order for detention by the collector along with the ground of detention as well as intimation that the detenu had a right to make a representation within a specified time. He then turned to the man, asking him to come the next day at 10 am. Having sent off the man, he asked me to draft and finalize the representation by that evening. I came back home, got ready and left for Mr Patnaik's office instead of going to the high court. I read some of the case laws and also went through the annotated edition of the Preventive Detention Act and started writing the representation. I finished my notes around 5 pm, and met Mr Patnaik around 6:30 pm at his office. He went through my handwritten draft, made some minor corrections and told me to get the draft typed and to leave it on his office table. When the stenographer came, I finished that job and left it on the office table of Mr Patnaik. Engrossed in this work, I could not attend the office of Mr Pal that evening too. I felt guilty for not being able to intimate him of my absence.

The next morning, after a quick stop at court, I reached Mr Patnaik's office around 9 am and found the man from the previous day already waiting there. When he met me, he handed me Rs 1500. I went inside and told Mr Patnaik that the man had arrived and also gave him the money I received. Mr Patnaik, however, told me that the money was meant for me and asked me to call the man into his office. When the man came in, Mr Patnaik read out the draft, which was about five full-scape typed pages. He just read it for 10–15 minutes and then told me to make the necessary corrections. He then asked the man to submit his fees. When the man enquired about the amount, he immediately quoted Rs 5000. I was surprised to find that the man promptly paid up. Mr Patnaik also told him to give Rs 500 each to the clerk and stenographer, to which he also complied. He then told me to show him the corrected draft after it was finally typed before handing it over to the client. When the draft was finally typed, I showed it to him, he glanced through it and told me to hand it over to the client. Then he enquired as to whether I had taken any food or not. On my saying no, he ordered food for both of us so that I could accompany him to the court thereafter. While eating food with him, I thought to myself that for this job I might have hardly made Rs 100–200 in the office of Mr Pal, and so Rs 1,500 for writing a representation was certainly beyond my imagination. I also thought that at this rate, our Kafla house would be completed much sooner.

One morning shortly thereafter, I met Mr Pal and told him that I would discontinue with him, as I planned to set up my independent practice, though for some time I would continue with Mr Patnaik. He never asked me any reason and offered his copious blessings. He said that if at any time I needed his help or advice, his office would always be open to me. I expressed my gratitude to him, and as I left his office, I was flooded with many sweet memories.

Even though I had taken up a space on rent with the intention of starting my independent practice, I continued working with Mr Patnaik for about four-and-a-half years, till the summer of 1971. He got so many cases during that period that I remained awfully busy all the time. The upside was that I gained considerable experience in constitutional law and criminal law while working with him. His method of preparation for cases was quite different. He took only a few cases, but he was very thorough and charged high fees, possibly the highest fees in Orissa High Court Bar. So, juniors attached to him used to earn handsomely too.

Mr Patnaik bore all the hallmarks of a successful lawyer. He was well-read, hardworking and diligent. I remember a case relating to the service conditions of Bihar and Orissa employees and their retirement. The question for consideration was whether a provision of the Bihar and Orissa Service Code would apply to them or the Orissa Service Code alone would apply to them, since they had been absorbed as employees of the Government of Orissa, when Orissa became a separate state on 1 April 1936. Initially the matter was heard before the two-judge bench, and the two judges gave a split view. The matter was then placed before the chief justice for constituting a larger bench. Instead of constituting a three-judge bench, which was the common practice, he constituted a five-judge bench to be presided over by himself. The newly constituted bench also included the two judges who had given the split verdict. Amongst the judges there were three service judges and two bar judges, including the chief justice himself.

Mr Patnaik was engaged for the petitioner and continued his arguments, but the chief justice was not agreeing with his views. By the end of the second day, I thought there was no hope for us. That evening when I gave my impression to Mr Patnaik, he immediately said that he was sanguine and optimistic based on his arguments in court and the position of the law as it stood that the petitioners must succeed. Further research was conducted that evening and by about midnight, I could lay my hands on two–three other Supreme Court decisions supporting the argument of Mr Patnaik. He told me to leave the reference on his bedside table so he would be able to review it early in the morning. When I reached his house early the next morning, he thanked me profusely for those references. He said that the three decisions I had found and researched would definitely change the attitude of the chief justice.

That afternoon, the tenacity with which Mr Patnaik could persuade the chief justice, encouraging him to read the three decisions by the Supreme Court on similar subjects was remarkable. By about 3 pm, the chief justice was convinced and changed his opinion in our favour. He then called upon the state counsel to argue. From the discussion, it appeared that except for one judge the other four were in our favour. The arguments were finally closed the next day, and when the judgement was delivered, there was a split of 3 vs 2, and we won the case. The majority judgement had been written by the chief justice himself.

I assisted Mr Patnaik in many such important cases during my tenure in his office between 1967–71. Besides being an excellent lawyer, Mr Patnaik was also very affectionate towards the juniors attached to his office and concerned about their well-being. He even ensured that all his juniors were paid sufficiently so that there would be no difficulty in managing their family expenses. He was also very friendly with all his juniors and always addressed them as his 'colleagues'. All the three advocates working with him became quite successful in their careers. Another lawyer who joined his office just before I left was A.K. Patnaik, who ultimately retired as a judge of the Supreme Court of India. Today, I can proudly say that it is by virtue of the training I got under him that I was able to find success in my career.

The construction work in our Kafla house was progressing with speed because of the augmented fees I was receiving in the office of Mr Patnaik. My mother's insistence on my marriage continued, and one day I became so vexed that I told her she could go ahead and fix my marriage with whoever she liked. With this reply from me, she fixed up my marriage sometime in March 1967 with the niece of Bipra Charan Das, who was a retired district judge widely known in the legal circle for being one of the most able and honest district judges the state had produced. In fact, the wife of my maternal uncle, who had arranged my appointment with Burmah Shell at Calcutta, was related to Bipra Charan Das, and in that connection, she had met the girl. So, she took my mother to meet the girl and the wedding was finalised for 23 June 1967. I was just informed of the decision by my mother; I was not given any other details nor shown a picture of my would-be bride.

In our family, one other marriage before mine was that of my eldest sister, way back in 1949. I still remember the grandeur with which it had been performed and how much money my father had spent. The village house had been especially electrified for her wedding with a generator brought in from Cuttack. There was a temporary telephone connection at the front door and a loudspeaker with recorded songs being played throughout the day. A huge congregation of villagers had gathered to watch the wedding procession. My marriage was taking place 18 years later, but my father was just as keen, notwithstanding his retirement from service, that it be performed in Cuttack with equal grandeur. We hired a bigger house in Cuttack itself, and made all the arrangements for the marriage there. On the evening of 23 June 1967, many senior lawyers and my friends, apart from our relatives, joined the barat. Since a marriage in the family was going to be performed after a long gap, our barat consisted of about 100 persons, and the number of cars were more than 40. The brand-new white Fiat car of Mr B.M. Patnaik was nicely decorated with flowers for the groom to ride in. My barat was so huge that special police had to be ordered to guide the traffic and people.

Even on the marriage pandal (altar), I could not see the face of the girl, since it was covered. Only her hand could be seen, and she seemed extremely thin. The wedding ritual started at midnight and went on for about four hours. It was monsoon, and it was drizzling all through the night. On the day after the marriage, Bipra Babu told me that I should not stop his niece's study and she should be allowed to complete her degree in Science. It was then that I was introduced to my wife's younger brother Devaduta (Tikan). I did not know till then about the family members of my wife apart from the fact that she had lost her father only a few years back. After my marriage, I also learnt that my wife, Meera, had a younger sister who was continuing her studies in a school and was staying in Bipra Babu's house. All these relocations in their family had occurred on account of her father's untimely death. My father-in-law's name was Kanungo Narendra Chandra Das. A native of Dharmagatpur, a few miles from Salepur, he worked at the state museum. For some time, he had also served in the army during the Second World War and was posted in Chittagong. And a few months after my marriage, my mother-in-law also passed away. Therefore, I counted Bipra Babu as my father-in-law and his wife as my mother-in-law.

In those days, the idea of a honeymoon trip was not prevalent in Orissa. A few months after our marriage, on my wife's insistence, I arranged to visit Puri for two days and made the necessary reservation in the forest bungalow at Puri. When I told my father about my visit to Puri, he initially said that it was not an auspicious day for going out, but reluctantly agreed with the rider that we should come back by the evening. So, our honeymoon trip only lasted from 7 am to 6 pm.

After our wedding, my wife and I continued living in our Oriya Bazar house, even though it was cramped. However, moving to some other rented accommodation was not possible at that time, as shifting to a rented house alone with my wife was not acceptable and my income was not sufficient to rent a big house where all of us could be accommodated. That apart, our house at Kafla was nearing completion, and so after some pleading, I could persuade my wife to continue in our Oriya Bazaar house for a little longer. It is here that my eldest son, Amar, was born on 15 April 1968. Being the first child in my family, Amar was thoroughly pampered.

Towards the end of 1968, our Kafla house was completed, though the boundary wall had not been constructed yet. My wife insisted that we should shift to our own house immediately, as we would have more space besides electricity and water. The house consisted of four big rooms, a kitchen and dining space, a store room and two bathrooms. Finally, in March 1969, we moved into our own house in Kafla. It took some time for me to adjust to our new surroundings. There was definitely more space. We had one bedroom for every nuclear family unit, my parents, my brother and his wife, and me and my family. The kitchen, dining area and hall remained common. From the new house, it was even easier for me to commute to the court, since my friend D.P. Mahapatra stayed in the same locality and had started going to court by car. He would give me a ride to and from the court daily.

Within two years of moving, my second son, Anjan, was born on 10 April 1970, and towards the end of the year, President's Rule had been promulgated in Orissa. S. Mohanty was the advocate general then. In those days, the office of the advocate general had provisions for three law officers—the advocate general himself, the government advocate and the standing counsel. Later, two posts of additional standing counsel were created, but they were only to assist the law officers and were not given any independent charge. P.K. Dhal was the standing counsel and N.K. Das was the government advocate at the time. When Mr Dhal resigned, the post of standing counsel became vacant. Now, normally the law officers are appointed by the political party in power, but as the state was under President's Rule, the appointment of law officer could only be made with the concurrence of the chief justice of the high court. Mr Mohanty, the advocate general, was keen to appoint his own junior for that post. It seems, however, that when the file reached Chief Justice G.K. Mishra, he suggested my name to the advocate general and requested him to appoint me. I was then called to the office of Chief Justice Mishra, where he informed me of this development and told me that I should not refuse this appointment, reasoning that even though the pay was less, it was a prestigious opportunity for me.

When I informed Mr B.M. Patnaik of this development, he frankly told me that he had become so dependent on me over the last four years that he would face immense difficulty in the event I left his office. Mr Patnaik had three other young advocates as his juniors at that point, Kedarnath Jena, Manoranjan Panda and Subhash Lal, but somehow, he relied on me the most. Nevertheless, he said that he would never stand in the way of my career progression. When I told my father, he was extremely pleased, but left the decision-making to me. I thought over the matter seriously and went ahead and joined the office of the advocate general, especially since Chief Justice Mishra had himself recommended my name for the post.

# Tenure at the Office of the Advocate General

I joined the office of the advocate general as standing counsel in early 1971. During my time, apart from the advocate general, S. Mohanty, and the government advocate, N.K. Das, there were the two additional standing counsels, D.P. Rath and Ghanshyam Sahu. I was in charge of criminal cases for which no extra fees were paid, but by the grace of the advocate general, I was getting some civil matters for which extra payment was available, and I used to make about Rs 900 per month, which was not even half of the money I was making when attached to the office of Mr Patnaik. By that time, my family had grown. That apart our instalment payment for the house loan was still continuing. As such I was facing a financial crunch, but the consolation was that I got the opportunity of meeting many well-known criminal lawyers not only from Orissa High Court but also the lawyers who had come from outside the state. To name a few, there was Ashok Sen who was the law minister with the Government of India. He had come to argue for bail in the famous bomb blast case that had taken place near our Oriya Bazaar house, and bail was refused. Mr Baroda Pyne from Calcutta had argued for the accused in the murder case but lost the case. Mr Sidharth Shankar Ray appeared in a pending original suit before the civil judge at Bhubaneswar and wanted production of certain documents. On behalf of the department of state government, privilege had been claimed. I was specially engaged to argue that privilege application, and ultimately my argument was upheld. The matter was brought to the high court, where Mr Ray himself appeared, and the advocate general argued for the state, with me assisting, and ultimately, we won the case.

After the President's Rule ended, the elected government under the leadership of Biswanath Das came into power, and R.C. Mishra was appointed as the advocate general. Mr Mishra was basically a criminal lawyer who had been practising in the district court at Berhampur and later on shifted his practice to Cuttack. He was quite well-versed in criminal law as well as civil law, and I assisted him on constitutional matters. However, the government headed by Biswanath Das was short-lived, and was followed by a Congress government under the leadership of Nandini Satpathy. Gangandhar Rath was appointed as advocate general. During my entire tenure of about 11 years in the office of the advocate general, Mr Rath was the advocate general for the longest period in three different terms.

I worked on many interesting cases in my career as standing counsel, and remember some of them quite vividly. One morning, as I was preparing to leave for court, I received a telephone call. To my surprise, the caller was Padma Nabh Mishra, the then home secretary to Government of Orissa. He informed me that he wanted to meet me at my residence in connection with some urgent work. I had no other option but to tell him to come down to my Kafla house. In about 15–20 minutes, he reached my house. When I asked him the reason for such urgency, he informed me that he had come to me to discuss the matter of parole of D.B.M. Patnaik, which was listed on the agenda of the court that day and I was supposed to appear for the state government. D.B.M. Patnaik was an advocate practising at Gunpur, his home town. He had been kept in jail on account of some allegation of Naxalite activity, and while in jail, his son had committed suicide for which a parole application had been made. Mr Mishra then told me that the chief minister (CM), Mrs Satpathy, was desirous of getting Mr Patnaik's parole granted, but the instruction from the government was in the negative, with a detailed report about Mr Patnaik's Naxalite activity, describing him as one of the deadliest Naxalites who should never be released. In those days, the Naxalite movement was quite active, particularly in Bengal. Mr Mishra's confession made my job easy, since I was of the same view, so I told him that I would tell the court that government had no objection if parole was granted. But there was a problem, the home secretary replied that if parole was granted on the CM's request, the Indira Gandhi government would replace her the next day. Therefore, the job had to be done tactfully so that it would appear the government protested and yet the court granted the parole. Since I was the standing counsel, who was the third law officer in rank, I told the home secretary that it was beyond my power and maybe the advocate general could help. I then accompanied the home secretary to the residence of the advocate general, Mr Rath. However, he, too, said that he would not be able to argue the matter and I should submit before the court whatever I thought was best. On our way to court, I told Mr Mishra that in such a sensitive matter it may not be appropriate to concede that parole be granted.

Having reached the court, we rushed to the court of Justice K.B. Panda before whom the matter had been listed. The counsel for the petitioner was Mr Prabir Palit, who was also a member of Communist Party of India and a friend of Mr Patnaik. He argued that parole should be granted on humanitarian consideration. The court asked for my response. I began submitting about his Naxalite activities, which had been given to me by the government. Mr Palit then interjected that the state counsel should take instructions from the government. The court, therefore, adjourned the matter till the next day. I found the home secretary waiting in my chamber when I returned from court during mid-day recess. He further told me that under no circumstances could the government give instruction in writing that the petitioner should be granted parole but urged me to find a way for the sake of the CM and left my office.

In the evening, Mr Rath rang me up and requested me to meet him at his residence. It was possible that the CM had told him about this case. I took the file with me and met the advocate general at his residence. He went through the file for about half an hour and told me that I would have to submit the case without conceding in the matter. Returning home, I thought over the matter for quite some time and drafted what I would submit. I remember the same till today and my draft went like this: 'Having regard to the past antecedents of the petitioner, he ought not to get parole. But since his son has died by suicide, on humanitarian consideration, the court may direct that he should be taken to his home in Gunpur and be kept in Gunpur jail till the 11th day. His family members can meet him in jail as per jail rule between 10 am and 4 pm, and family means his wife and children. On the 11th day, he would be taken to his home, which will be encircled by police force, and he would be made free to perform the rituals. Before 4 pm, he should be brought back to Gunpur Jail and then taken to the jail from which he had been brought.' I asked my stenographer to make three copies of the same to be kept in relevant files.

On the next day, this was the very first case in the court. As soon as the case was called, I stood up and handed over one copy to the court and other to Mr Palit, and kept the third copy in my hand. The presiding judge went through the same and observed that it was a very fair submission. Mr Palit wanted some modification to which I did not agree. Ultimately, the court dictated the order but instead of the court directing it, the order was 'Learned standing counsel submits and accordingly I direct.' Possibly the judge did not want to take the sole responsibility on himself. I, however, did not protest. When I reached my chamber at 1 pm, I found the home secretary waiting in my room. He got up to congratulate me and convey his thanks and told me that the CM was really pleased with the outcome. Before leaving my room, as a token of thanks, he offered to arrange accommodation for me at the Utkal Bhawan at Calcutta or Orissa Bhawan at Delhi whenever I needed it. Getting accommodation in both the places was a really difficult job those days, and Mr Mishra delivered on his promise every time I approached him.

However, the matter wasn't closed even after a court order for parole. That afternoon, I received at least 4–5 telephone calls from high-ranking police officers asking me as to why parole had been granted, for, according to them, Mr Patnaik was a dangerous man at risk of flight. Even the last telephone call I got from the inspector general of police was to the same effect, to which I replied, 'If our police are so inefficient, better we should not have the force.' The consequence of this reply was that the Intelligence branch gave a report against me stating, 'Has strong leaning towards Naxalite, helped dreaded Naxalite leader D.B.M. Patnaik.' This I discovered only in 1983 when my name was recommended for the position of a judge of Orissa High Court.

During my tenure of about 11 years in the advocate general's office, from April 1971 till June 1983, I worked with six advocate generals. S. Mohanty was the advocate general during President's Rule, when I was first appointed; R.C. Mishra during the chief ministership of Biswanath Das; Gangadhar Rath during the chief ministership of Nandini Satpathy; B.M. Patnaik during the chief ministership of Nilamani Routray;

Govind Das during the chief ministership of J.B. Patnaik, but he did not continue for the full term; and Gangadhar Rath was appointed to the post again sometime in 1982. I developed a good rapport with each of the advocate generals.

While Mr Rath was still advocate general, N.K. Das, the government advocate, was elevated as a judge of the high court, and B.B. Mohanty was appointed to the post. Two posts of additional government advocate were created, and Mr Rath called me to his residence and told me that he would like to get Mr D.P. Mahapatra as additional government advocate number one and I should be appointed as additional government advocate number two. He then explained that there was no seniority or any additional benefit, but since Mr Mahapatra was senior to me in age and also in practice, he should be appointed as additional government advocate number one. I immediately responded that I would resign if I was not made the additional government advocate number one, as having served in his office for a length of time, I had a better claim on the post. Without any hesitation, he immediately agreed with me. As additional government advocate, we became entitled to fees while arguing civil matters on the basis of the valuation of dispute. In arguing writ cases, the fee was Rs 100 per day, the income thus became quite handsome and, on an average, I was earning more than Rs 60,000 per annum.

During this period, one interesting case that comes to my mind is connected to one Dinanath Pansari who had an automobile business. Under the orders of the collector, his business premises had been searched and it was found that there was one tyre in excess for which no explanation could be given. The collector issued an order of detention under the provisions of Maintenance of Internal Security Act (MISA), but the order could not be effected as the detenue was shielding himself somewhere. It was about 10 months after that the detenue was arrested by virtue of the said order. The district collector of Keonjhar was one Pyari Mohan

Mahapatra. The detenue filed a writ petition challenging his detention, and it was listed before the bench of Justice R.N. Mishra and Justice N.K. Das. I was in charge of that court. The matter was to come up on Monday. On Friday evening, Pyari Mohan Mahapatra and S.M. Patnaik, deputy secretary in the home department that was dealing with the detention matter, reached my residence. I had known both of them from earlier, and Mr Mahapatra told me that this case had to be won at any cost. While they were in my office, I read the brief cursorily and told them that it was not possible to win this case. Mr Mahapatra told me that even if we lose, he would challenge the same in the Supreme Court. I just posed him one question as to how was he so convinced that Mr Pansari should be detained under the relevant act. I also asked him why the order could not be executed for more than 10 months. He replied that the detenue had taken shelter in the residence of a high-ranking police officer. I then asked if he would able to file an affidavit to that effect, but he replied that it was not possible. Then I thought it would be better if the advocate general, Mr Rath, argued this case. But when we took up the matter with him, the advocate general refused on grounds that he was travelling. While leaving, Mr Mahapatra also informed me that Mr Pansari was probably in touch with the judges presiding over the case. In the circumstances, I assured Mr Mahapatra that I would certainly argue the case to the best of my ability, but that chances of success were slim. I studied the brief for two full days and made notes in my notebook, including relevant case laws. The detenue was being represented by Barrister Ranjit Mohanty and R.C. Patnaik. Mr Patnaik was junior in the office of Justice R.N. Mishra and was also a great favourite of Justice N.K. Das.

The case was called around noon, and Mr Mohanty took about 45 minutes to conclude his submission. When I got up to argue, I was asked by the bench as to how long I would take. Instead of giving any definite time, I replied that the case would take some time. The bench got annoyed and told me, 'Only 1 hour is granted.' I, however, replied that I could not promise that I would conclude my submission within an hour, when the court rose for lunch. After lunch, the courtroom was fully packed. It was my habit to be adamant if any court would stand in my way of arguing a case, and especially if the approach of the court was improper. I began the case at 2 pm, and just after 1 hour, when the bench remarked that the hour was over, I immediately stated, 'My lords, I feel I am not being allowed to argue.' The judges became annoyed and sat quietly. By the end of the day, when the court rose at 4 pm, I mentioned that I had not finished half of my argument and thus it would take me at least one more day. The presiding judge then immediately told me that on the next day I should give the argument in writing. I came back home with Mr Mahapatra and Mr Patnaik, the Deputy Secretary of the home department, and after having a cup of tea with them at my house, called my stenographer and started dictating my argument for the next day. The written argument was about 60 pages, and I told my stenographer to prepare the final typescript and make three copies of it. It was about 10 pm when Mr Mahapatra and Mr Patnaik left for Bhubneshwar.

The next day, this was the first case in the list and as soon as the court started, I handed over the notes to the judges and gave one copy to the advocate for petitioner. Seeing the notes to be quite heavy, Justice Mishra, the presiding judge, told me that they would read the notes at home. I immediately replied that since not even half my argument was presented, either I should get the opportunity of reading my notes or be permitted to argue orally. The court then asked me to read the notes. As soon as I started reading out my arguments, the opposition lawyers raised objections saying the arguments were fallacious. In reply I backed all my arguments with relevant decisions of the Supreme Court. In this manner, by the lunch interval, only about 20 pages of the note had been read. When the court rose for lunch, the presiding judge told me that instead of reading the note I should argue orally. I readily agreed, saying that I would argue in whichever format the court wanted as long as I was not prevented from my right of arguing.

My argument continued after lunch, and by about 3 pm, the presiding judge posed a question to me: 'Mr Government Advocate, supposing your collector searches my house and finds one tyre extra, will you advise your collector to issue an order under MISA?' I could not think of an answer immediately, but after some thought, I said, 'My Lord, your lordship is not a dealer under tyre control order and not doing any business, but assuming you satisfy the definition of dealer and your premises is searched and one extra tyre is found, looking at your status, the collector may not be satisfied that the situation needs invocation of MISA! But if the collector is satisfied and issues an order of detention, the court cannot interfere in exercise of power under Article 226 of the Constitution, and this is all I want to impress upon.' The face of the judge became red and thereafter he did not utter a single word. I continued my submission, and just 10 minutes before 4 pm, I finished my argument and apologised to the judge. The court then asked the counsel of the petitioner for a reply, and he answered that no reply was necessary. I realised that the two judges were entirely in favour of the detenue, and therefore, the question of giving any reply was not necessary. I was certain that the case was lost.

Six weeks later, the judgement was delivered and, to my great surprise, I found that judges had accepted each of my submissions and dismissed the petition of the detenue. I remembered on that day a famous saying of my senior Mr B.K. Pal, 'Every case has its luck.'

Later I learnt that Dinanath Pansari had appealed in the Supreme Court. I remember how, one stormy afternoon, while I was on leave from court and resting at home due to some ailment, Pyari Mohan Mahapatra and S.M. Patnaik came to my house and requested me to prepare a counter affidavit and go the Delhi for the purpose. Since I was ill, I told them that they should proceed to Delhi and an advocate on record would file the necessary affidavit and a senior advocate could be engaged to argue the matter, but they did not agree. My friend Mr Mahapatra told me that I should not leave him halfway through, to which I replied that I would prepare the counter affidavit but the question of my going to Delhi did not arise. Next day evening, all the paperwork were handed over to me and even though I was burning with fever, I called my stenographer and prepared the counter affidavit. Since I myself had argued the case, it did not take much time to prepare the counter affidavit. On the next evening, they both again came to my house to collect the counter affidavit and thanked me no end. They also proceeded to Delhi and filed the same. Two days thereafter, the case had been listed, and the Supreme Court dismissed the application. Mr Mahapatra rang me up from the court itself to express his thanks.

It is on that day I realised how valid the advice and request of the chief justice was when he asked me to join as standing counsel in the office of the advocate general. During my four–five years as standing counsel, I had built for myself such a reputation that senior officers of the government used to request the advocate general that I should argue their case. Generally, government lawyers do not come prepared to court, as they feel that they have no involvement in the case. But during my time, I would never go to court without preparation and used to devote a lot of time to reading the case brief.

After Mr Rath, B.M. Patnaik was appointed the advocate general sometime in 1977, during the chief ministership of Nilamani Routray. At that time, B.B. Mohanty was continuing as the government advocate. But when for some reason, the government did not agree for Mr Mohanty's renewal, on the recommendation of the advocate general, I was appointed as the government advocate, at just 38 years old. Mr Patnaik had so much trust in me that he handed me the entire responsibility of the office of the advocate general. That apart I also got several opportunities to represent the state in the Supreme Court. On an average, I used to be in Delhi for almost 10–12 days a month. I had lot of friends in Delhi, and thus, evenings were spent with them either in Orissa Bhavan itself or in some hotel. My friends from that time included Nilamadhab Mohanty, R.K. Bhujabal, M.P. Modi, J.P. Das and others.

During that period, I also came in contact with many senior lawyers of the Supreme Court. It was indeed a great pleasure and satisfaction to argue before the learned judges of the Supreme Court, particularly when your contentions were accepted by the court. I remember that once during summer vacation, I was in Delhi in connection with some other case in the Supreme Court, and our advocate on record, Mr Parth Sharthi, sent a brief that had been listed for grant of special leave before the vacation judge on a taxation matter. When I saw that brief at about 8 pm, I immediately rang up Mr Parth Sharthi and told him that he might engage some other senior counsel since I was not very conversant with taxation matter. He replied over telephone that the point involved was rather simple, namely whether a 'fishing net' would come under a particular entry as held by the high court in the impugned judgement or some other entry as contended by the state. He also said that it was difficult to find senior counsel on account of vacation. Instead of wasting any further time, I just started reading the brief, and within an hour, could sort out how I would represent the matter the next day. Justice Shingal was very strict in the grant of special leave, and our matter was at serial number 11. All the matters from 1–10 had been dismissed. I was really nervous when my matter was called. To my great surprise, as soon as I told the court about the point involved, within two minutes, special leave was granted and the order of the high court was stayed. When I came out of the courtroom, a very senior lawyer from Calcutta, who was standing outside, expressed his surprise and said that such a quick verdict from Justice Singhal called for a celebration. I took him to the canteen and offered him a cup of tea, while he regaled me with stories from the courtroom of Justice Singhal.

Another memorable case in Orissa High Court was when M.R. Panda, who was junior in the office of B.M. Patnaik, was arguing a case listed for final hearing that involved a chowkidar in a company, who had been dismissed from service as he was found to have taken liquor in course of duty. The division bench consisted of G.K. Mishra, the chief justice, and his companion Justice B.K. Patra. Right from the beginning, the CJ was against the petitioner, and he was not permitting him to argue. The brother judge was sympathetic to the counsel but kept quiet on account of the Chief Justice. After some time, the CJ interjected, 'Mr Panda, you don't know, once you are drunk how will you behave?' B.M. Patnaik, who was also present in the court and was listening quietly all this while, suddenly stood up and addressed the CJ, 'My Lord, I take drinks regularly and, your lordships, see where I am.' This changed the mind of the court. Mr Panda was allowed to make his submissions and the counsel for the company/employer responded. Ultimately, the court held that the punishment of dismissal was wholly disproportionate to the offence committed, and therefore, the order of dismissal was set aside and instead the punishment of stopping two annual increments was imposed. For the period of absence, no salary was made available. The purpose of my mentioning this incident is to stress that fact the judge is also a human being, and therefore, his personal impression or bias also affects the fate of a case, however impartial he may be.

An important case relating to my period as a government advocate during the tenure of B.M. Patnaik as advocate general was one where former CM Mrs Nandini Satpathy was being prosecuted by the state vigilance department in a case of disproportionate assets. Her application for bail was before the district judge of Cuttack. In course of search of her premises, a diary of her son had been seised that mentioned many events concerning the character of Mrs Satpathy. As the advocate general was away in Delhi, I was required to argue the matter. The vigilance DSP, Mr Patel, who was the investigating officer, told me that the said diary be placed before the court, as desired by then CM, Nilamani Routray. I read a couple of pages from the diary and found that said diary had absolutely no relevance to the case in hand. The only purpose being served by its use was the character assassination of Mrs Satpathy. So, I refused to place the diary before the court. The investigating officer must have conveyed this to the CM. In evening, the chief minster called me to his residence. Even there, I tried to impress upon him that the diary was not relevant to the case, but the CM answered, 'You are a young man, and you will not understand the importance of the diary. If you are not willing to place the diary, then take an adjournment from court, and the advocate general will argue the matter on his return from Delhi.' I assured the CM that I would take an adjournment. By the time I reached home, I was informed by my wife that the advocate general had called me from Delhi twice. Shortly thereafter, yet another call came from him, and when I discussed the matter with him, he, too, asked me to take an adjournment. When the case was called the next day, the counsel for Mrs Satpathy wanted to argue, however, as directed, I requested the case be adjourned for one day. Without any hesitation, the judge adjourned the case. The advocate general returned from Delhi and argued the case. In course of his argument, he not only placed the diary but also read in court several pages that were grossly derogatory, and all the local newspapers flashed the excerpts with headlines. Ultimately, of course, the bail was granted, but the adverse publicity in the newspapers affected the reputation of Mrs Satpathy. CM Routray must have derived political advantage from that. I, however, cannot but praise the attitude and the thinking of the CM, the reason being notwithstanding his request and that of the advocate general, even though I, as a government advocate, remained adamant in not placing a document that I thought to be unnecessary, the CM never kept any grudge on that score. Not only did he extend my tenure by one more term as a government advocate but later he also forwarded my name for elevation as a judge of the high court in the year 1979 when I was hardly 41 years old. Obviously, this proves his broad-mindedness.

While I was the government advocate in the office of the advocate general, I had defended the state government in several arbitral proceedings. There was one arbitration proceeding relating to supply of rice in the district of Kalahandi, and a gentleman whom I knew as Mr Shastri was giving us necessary papers for being filed before the arbitrator. He was from the civil supply department. One afternoon, when I returned from the court to my office room at around 4 pm, I found Mr Shastri waiting for me there. I ordered for two cups of tea, and while sipping tea, he took my right hand and examined it for about 15 minutes. Thereafter he told me that there would be a change of profession in my life when I would reach 45 years of age. He also told me that I did not have any fate line but that on account of my wife's fate line, I would rise quite high in life and earn substantially but would never be able to have much savings, as was similarly predicted by a relative of mine in my childhood. I casually told him that in this profession the question of any change did not arise. He, however, insisted that there would be a change when I would reach 45 years of age. I have no faith either in palmistry or in astrology. But the subsequent events of my life have played out just as Mr Shastri had predicted.

Sometime in December 1978, while Mr B.M. Patnaik was continuing as advocate general, around 1 pm, while I was signing some official file in my room, I was summoned by the then chief justice of Orissa High Court, S.K. Ray. I was surprised to get this call as I was arguing before the chief justice right from 10:30 am till noon that very same morning. I thought to myself that possibly I made some mistake in the case. As soon as I reached his chamber, he asked me to take a seat and enquired from me as to whether any other advocate has seen me coming to his chamber, and I answered in the negative. Then he asked me to submit a copy of my income tax return of last three years and also a letter of consent indicating that I would accept the job of a judge if appointed. Then he frankly told me that he wanted to recommend my name for appointment as a judge of Orissa High Court. I came back from his chamber and then after the court hours, got to arranging the documents. I compiled all those papers in an envelope and returned home late. When my wife asked why I was so late I only stated that I was busy on account of some official work.

S.K. Ray had been the chief justice for more than a year by then, but I had never visited him either in his residence or even in his official chamber on a courtesy call. I had no relationship with him while he was at the Bar apart from my presence in court by way of defending the state government in his court almost daily. I was surprised that Justice Ray would consider me suitable for the prestigious position at that young age of 41. Until then, no lawyer in Orissa had been elevated at such a young age. I considered this opportunity a blessing of the family deity, Lord Radhakanth Dev, and one that came my way on account of my wife's luck. Finally, my long-held dream of living in a bungalow, as was allotted to judges during those days, would come true. However, on the next day, after reaching the high court, when I went to the chamber of the Justice Ray and gave him the papers he had requested, he enquired as to whether Advocate R.C. Patnaik had seen me on the previous day when I had been called to his chamber. I was surprised at this question and replied in the negative. He then told me that immediately after I had left his chamber on the previous day, Mr Patnaik had met him in his chamber. Justice Ray asked me not to disclose this fact to anybody, not even to my wife, and I complied with his instruction faithfully.

Few days thereafter, a query had been made from the CJI as to whether the income shown by me in three previous years was the professional income or income from some other sources. I was given a copy of that query and was told submit a reply to the CJI the next day. I did make the draft indicating that except for about Rs 300 as remuneration for being examiner in a law exam rest was professional income. During those three years, the average income I had shown was about Rs 1,20,000 per annum, and that income was considered to be quite high since the salary of a judge was only Rs 42,000 per annum. After about a month, a further query had been made by the CJI, as to why such a young advocate had been chosen for elevation as a judge to the high court. The answer given by the chief justice of Orissa High Court was not known to me then, which I got to know only in 1995, when I was acting chief justice of Orissa High Court: 'I have consulted two persons in the age group 50–60, the present advocate general and the former advocate general, and both of them declined. Between the age group of 40–50, I have considered four advocates, namely R.C. Patnaik, G.B. Patnaik, L. Rath and D.P. Mohapatra. And I selected G.B. Patnaik considering his ability, performance in courts, honesty and integrity.'

In the meanwhile, Advocate General B.M. Patnaik went ahead with recommending the renewal of my tenure as the government advocate for a further period of three years. But the CM informed him that my name had been recommended for the post of a judge of Orissa High Court. But on the insistence of Mr Patnaik, my tenure as government advocate was extended for another three years. Almost about a month thereafter, the advocate general on his return from Delhi told me that he had received information that the CJI had approved my name, and the file had been sent to the PM for his approval. He also told me that the vacancy would arise only in July, and therefore, the notification may come by the end of June 1979.

In March 1979, Charan Singh, the then home minister to the Government of India in the Morarji Desai cabinet was visiting Orissa. A state dinner was hosted in his honour by the governor in Raj Bhawan. The judges of the high court were also invited to that dinner. While six or seven judges of Orissa High Court were having a discussion among themselves in one corner of the dining hall in Raj Bhawan, Mr Biju Patnaik, who was then the minister of steel in the Government of India, walked up to them and asked, 'Where is the new judge, young Patnaik?' The judges kept quiet since there was no Patnaik as judge at that point of time. But after that, Justice R.N. Mishra, the senior-most judge, and Justice N.K. Das went straight to the residence of R.C. Patnaik with packets of sweets and congratulated him on the assumption that it was he who was to be appointed as a judge. Next morning, when I reached the high court premises, I found sweets were being distributed not only among lawyers but also to clients. Upon query, I was told that Mr Patnaik was distributing the sweets to celebrate his appointment as judge. I met Mr Patnaik and also congratulated him and went to the court after partaking of the sweets.

Two days thereafter, it was finally revealed it was not him. He approached the secretary to the governor, one R.C. Pal Singh, and found out that it was G.B. Patnaik, me. Having come to know that my name had been sponsored, a Bar Association meeting was called, which was presided over by Gangandhar Rath, the former advocate general. The main organiser to convene the meeting was Barrister Ranjit Mohanty, but the architect behind the scene was Justice R.N. Mishra. R.C. Patnaik, who lived near my house, even came to my house around midnight just before the scheduled meeting of the Bar, just to find out whether my name had been sponsored. I replied in affirmative and he told me that he was not keen on becoming a judge and that he would say so openly in the scheduled meeting the next day. In the meeting, however, except 14–15 young lawyers, everybody spoke against my elevation. The advocates who were opposing my elevation did so from various angles. There were many advocates who were desirous of becoming a judge themselves, so naturally, they were against me. There were many senior advocates who wanted to please the future chief justice, namely the senior-most judge of the high court, R.N. Mishra. There were few advocates who thought that it was at the behest of Advocate General B.M. Patnaik that Chief Justice Ray had sent my name, and those advocates were anti Mr Patnaik. The Bar Association passed a resolution to the effect that since the law commission had indicated that ordinarily a lawyer should be 45 years of age for being elevated as judge, my recommendation was invalid. Not only that but also a delegation of about six–seven lawyers, including R.C. Patnaik himself, went to Delhi, with the air tickets being paid for by a businessman named Ganga Ram Chapoliya on the instruction of Justice R.N. Mishra. When the delegation failed in their attempt to forestall the appointment, they met PM Morarji Desai and impressed upon him that the said candidate (me) was a young man addicted to drinks as well as a womanizer, and therefore, should not be elevated as a judge. The PM, without any further enquiry, prevailed upon the law minister, Mr Shanti Bhushan, and asked him to request the CJI to withdraw the recommendation. The CJI was initially not agreeable but later withdrew his recommendation by stating, 'I had reluctantly agreed with the recommendation of the chief justice of Orissa High Court. G.B. Patnaik is young. He should wait for some more time.' With this letter from the then CJI, Y.V. Chandrachud, the proposal of my elevation as a judge in the year 1979 came to an end.

I was in Delhi on that particular day when this became known, and our advocate on record, R.K. Mehta, then told me in the evening that even though I had refused a drink offered by him on several occasions in the past I must take a drink now, since, in the opinion of the prime minster of the country, I was a drunkard. I immediately agreed, and he prepared a drink which tasted more like sherbet, being concocted from gin, lime juice, soda and cherry. That scene is still fresh in my mind and will remain so till my death. Years later while I was a judge of the Supreme Court, at a farewell dinner organised at the India Habitat Centre on the occasion of the retirement of one of the judges of the Supreme Court, I found former CJI Y.V. Chandrachud sitting on a table with a drink. I sat by his side and paid my respects. He then asked me whether I had taken a drink or not. I answered that earlier to 1979, I was a teetotaller, as I never liked the taste, but something happened in that year that made me take a drink occasionally. He laughed heartily and told me that he still remembered the incident and clarified that he was not responsible for the same. I was surprised at his sharp memory at such an advanced age, given it had been 25 years since that incident by then.

I was not disturbed by the fact that I could not be elevated as a judge of the high court, but I was very much disturbed that a few members of the Bar maliciously and falsely distorted my character before the prime minster of India. I was further surprised that the PM of a country, without any further enquiry, acted on the statement of a small group of people and took a final decision on the question of the appointment of a judge to the high court, which was a constitutional obligation of the PM of the country. I was also equally surprised by the curious behaviour of R.C. Patnaik, who met me at midnight and frankly told that he would indicate in the Bar Association meeting that he was not inclined to become a judge, would become a member of the delegation and a privy to the false accusations against my character. A few days thereafter, he wrote an article in the *Blitz* magazine with the headline "Junior Favoured as a Judge". According to that article, it was because of the then advocate general, in whose office I was a junior for five years, that my name had been recommended for elevation. Ironically, shortly thereafter, when R.N. Mishra was the chief justice of Orissa High Court, he recommended the name of R.C. Patnaik for elevation, and he was elevated as a judge.

During that period, Bhupendra Bose, an influential member of the then Jan Sangh party, met Mr B.M. Patnaik and impressed upon him that he would like to go to Delhi with some of his colleagues and meet Atal Bihari Bajpai, who was then a minister in Morarji Desai's cabinet, about the matter of my appointment. But Mr Patnaik dissuaded him on the ground that no political colour needed to be added to such a matter. Mr Patnaik knew that since the matter had been approved by the CJI, nothing would ultimately reverse the decision.

In the year 1976, on the request of my wife, I had purchased a piece of land on Lewis Road, Bhubaneswar, for a sum of Rs 15,000. That was the only self-acquired property after about 15 years of practice. During my time as a junior with Mr. B.M. Patnaik as well as after joining the office of the advocate general as standing counsel, though I was earning a handsome figure, I was not able to save much money, as I used to spend a considerable amount visiting different places in India like Darjeeling, Shimla and Kashmir, with my family in tow. The payment of instalment towards the loan we had taken for the construction of our Kafla house was still continuing. By then I had even come into possession of a second-hand Fiat car from Dr M.S. Khadanga, a famous surgeon in those days, who was going to United Kingdom for a year and wanted to dispose of his car. The car was maintained in a brand-new condition. I had taken my mother and kids on many memorable trips in that car. Gradually our family home in Kafla also became a bit crowded; my daughter Rinku was born in April 1975. My wife insisted on adding a few rooms to the house, but I had stalled it in the anticipation of my elevation as a judge, but when that did not fructify in 1979, I thought of constructing three rooms upstairs with two bathrooms. A major part of my professional income during that time was being spent for the construction of the first floor.

There was a change of political government in the year 1980, and J.B. Patnaik became the CM, replacing Mr Routray. With that, B.M. Patnaik was replaced by Govind Das as the Advocate General. During that period, Chief Justice Ray again sent my name from the Bar and recommended the name of Dr B.N. Mishra from amongst the district judges, but only Dr Mishra's appointment was approved. He took oath in the year 1981, by which time Chief Justice Ray had retired in November 1980, and Justice R.N. Mishra was appointed the chief justice of Orissa High Court. Dr B.N. Mishra was my professor in MS Law College, and I had great regard for him. He was also very fond of me, and later, after my elevation, we became very close. Even today I am in contact with his children, though Dr Mishra is no more.

While Mr Govind Das was advocate general, I also continued as government advocate and my friend D.P. Mahapatra continued as additional government advocate number one. Mr Das also entrusted major responsibilities on me, though the job of distribution of cases and court amongst the law officers was being done by himself. Invariably, I was allotted the court of Chief Justice R.N. Mishra and was being sent to Supreme Court in several important cases. I had been deputed a couple of times to appear before the Bachawat River Tribunal, and our advocate on record before the tribunal was Mrs Sunanda Bhandari. Mr Govind Das used to tell me that since I was in Delhi so often, I should meet the CJI and impress upon him the matter of my elevation, but I never came to it.

Summer break for the high court started on the 17 or 18 of May. My friend D.P. Mahapatra and I had planned a trip to Kashmir with our families. Around that time, the collection and sale of sal seeds had been taken over by Orissa Forest Corporation and one J.P. Lath, a known businessman, filed a civil suit before the subordinate judge Sambalpur and obtained an order of injunction against the corporation and its officers. By the time the order of injunction was passed, the court closed. The said order of injunction had shaken the Orissa Forest Corporation, the forest department as well as the government of Orissa to some extent. In fact, in the past, sal seeds had played a key role in Orissa politics. At this, Advocate General Das advised on telephone that steps be taken for getting the matter listed before the vacation judge so that an appropriate interim order could be obtained. We did not even have the certified copy of the order of injunction, though we had one typed copy. B.K. Behera was the vacation judge. I personally met him at his residence and narrated all the difficulties, and I requested for the case to be listed the next morning, to which he agreed. I then came back to my house and drafted a petition and, after getting it vetted by the advocate general, filed it in the court with the affidavit of the then secretary to the forest department. An undertaking was given stating that the certified copy of the order would be filed within one week. The matter was taken up for consideration by the judge around noon in the residential office of the vacation judge. Within five minutes of hearing the advocate general, the vacation judge granted ex-part interim stay of the order of injunction passed by the subordinate judge and granted us 10 days' time to file the certified copy. The officers of the government were very happy with that order. On the next day, we left for Srinagar by train, via Delhi, as planned.

Since our return journey from Jammu by train had not been confirmed, we decided to reach Delhi from Srinagar by air. In Delhi, when we reached Orissa Bhavan, where we were to put up until our train back home, I found the managing director of Shimlipal Corporation, Mr Kanungo, waiting for me. Upon enquiry, he revealed that sal seed case was being heard at the Supreme Court, and the hearing was in two days. Even though the advocate general was in Delhi for the last four days, the counter affidavit had not been filed, and everybody was waiting for my presence. I politely told him that I would be of no help, exhausted as I was from my travel. Mr Kanungo became really worried and said that without my assistance the advocate general was not in a position to prepare the counter affidavit. I then took advantage of the situation and told him that I would agree to do the necessary job only on one condition, namely that my entire expenses for my Kashmir trip be paid by the corporation. Without a second thought, he agreed. I freshened up quickly and had my breakfast and left for hotel Taj Mansingh, where the advocate general was staying, with Mr Kanungo.

When we reached the hotel, I found G.S. Chatterjee, our advocate on record, and his stenographer waiting there. I had a discussion with the advocate general and then proceeded with the drafting of the counter affidavit. It took me about five–six hours to complete my dictation, and I returned to Orissa Bhavan only around 8 pm. The affidavit was filed the next day, and the matter was listed day after. I borrowed a gown from Mr Chatterjee and with my blazer that I had carried for my Kashmir trip, I attended court along with the advocate general. The vacation judge after listening to the arguments of both parties made some interim arrangement but never interfered with the right of collection and sale of sal seeds. He gave a rider that proper account should be maintained.

Mr Kanungo and the other government officer were very satisfied with the order, and I submitted my bill on my return to Cuttack. True to his word, Mr Kanungo himself came to my house and delivered a cheque of Rs 2000, more than the entire expenses of my Kashmir trip. A lawyer sometimes earns in this manner.

During the tenure of Mr Govind Das as advocate general, once when I was in Delhi, CM J.B. Patnaik was there in Orissa Bhavan. I met him and asked him about my elevation. He told me frankly that he would meet Chief Justice R.N. Mishra and request him for the same. When I told him that he himself could send a recommendation contrary to the views of the Chief Justice, he said he would not act in such a manner, as he felt, the CJI would only act favourably (send) if the Chief Justice recommended my name. I then realised that it would be better to forget about the elevation. But whenever I met the father-in-law of J.K. Mohanty, R.K. Das, he used to tell me that he had been requesting for the same all along to the CM, therefore, he expected that the proposal would go through. Needless to mention, CM J.B. Patnaik had profound regard for R.K. Das who was related to him through his wife.

In the year 1982, sometime in the last week of November or first week of December, I had been to Delhi to represent the state government on some important matters, and I was in Delhi for three days. It so happened that all the four cases had been listed on a Monday for the bench presided over by the CJI. The cases were: i) provisional admission into postgraduate courses in the medical college, ii) selection and promotion from the state administrative service to Indian Administrative Service, iii) nationalisation of a portion of the highway, an order which was assailed before Orissa High Court by the private operators and they had lost and appealed to the Supreme Court. The fourth matter I do not specifically recollect but it was a matter relating to some service condition of employees of the commerce department and the inter-se seniority. In each of these matters the court had already issued notice, and therefore, I was supposed to argue on the question of issuance of interim direction. The senior advocates who had appeared for the petitioner in these cases, as far as I remember, were Mr Tarkunde, the then solicitor general who later became law minister for a short period, a number of senior counsels, including K.K. Venugopal in the transport matter, and the former attorney general Mr Gupte. Each of those matters was fiercely contested, and I had opposed for issuance of any interim direction, and I must have argued for more than an hour in all those matters. Ultimately, the CJI did not pass any interim order in any of those matters.

Instead of returning next day, I came back on Wednesday, and by the time I reached my office room in the high court, I was told by my stenographer that I should meet the Chief Justice R.N. Mishra, as he had been searching for me since the previous day. I rushed to his chamber, and as soon as I entered, he asked me about the cases I had argued before the CJI recently. I shared all the details with him. However, what he said next, left me speechless. He said that he himself had been to Delhi and met the CJI, who was enquiring as to why my name had not been recommended for elevation so far. The Chief Justice Mishra further stated that he had already sent my name for elevation, relying upon the consent letter I had given in 1979 as well as the income tax return documents I had submitted at that point of time. He further told me I should submit my recent income tax returns documents and also casually observed that since I would have a fairly long tenure, I should develop cordial relations with R.C. Patnaik, who had already been a judge for about a year, for smooth functioning of the high court.

The next day, I received a message from the office of the CM that he wanted to meet me in his office that same evening. At that point of time, I was driving my car by myself. However, on coming to know about my visit to CM, Mr B.M. Patnaik sent his chauffeur-driven car for my trip to the secretariat. As I entered the CM's chamber, he told me that there was a delay of four years with regards my elevation for which he was sorry. At any rate, according to him, God gives every individual the reward that is due at a time which the Almighty thinks proper. The CM told me that the file would be sent to the central government on the next day and also congratulated me, hoping for early elevation to the bench. After my meeting, on my way back from the secretariat in Bhubaneswar I was just thinking about one thing: how the very gentleman who had played an important role behind the scene in organising a protest in the Bar Association in the year 1979 was almost forced to recommend my name later. I came to learn at a later point of time that Chief Justice Mishra was about to be transferred to Karnataka High Court, and it is in that connection he had met the CJI and was also trying for his elevation to the Supreme Court. What a coincidence! Luckily for me, before he met the CJI, I had argued in the court of the CJI. This was nothing but sheer destiny, in my opinion.

That evening I remembered my mother very much, since in 1979, when I was almost on the verge of my elevation, I had prematurely promised to take her on a pilgrimage to Badrinath and Kedarnath once appointed as a judge. However, she passed away in December 1982, and her desire to see Badrinath and Kedarnath remained unfulfilled. It was her encouragement that made it possible for me to take up the legal profession, yet I could not share this happy news with her.

In the meanwhile, there was a change in the post of advocate general, even though J.B. Patnaik continued as CM. Gangandhar Rath was appointed as the new advocate general. I knew him very well, as I had worked with him in two early phases.

One case during this time is worth mentioning. For admission to postgraduate classes in medical college, several people had filed writ petitions, and they were heard and disposed of by common judgement against them, and I was representing the state in the high court. The students had moved the Supreme Court for grant of special leave, and in the very first case, the senior counsel was Mr Tarkunde, and the matter had been listed in the court of the CJI. The court had directed issuance of notice and further ordered that provisional admission be given to the petitioner. Thereafter several such petitions had been filed, and I was not required to be present every time, and Mr Parasharan was our senior counsel. But in every case, provisional admission order was being passed. In the event, one K.B. Verma, who was the secretary in the health department, landed in my house one day and told me that the way in which the Supreme Court was directing for provisional admission, the medical council of India would derecognize the degree, and urged upon me that rather than engage a senior counsel I should appear for the state and impress upon the court the effect which the authorities apprehend on account of such provisional admission order.

Two days thereafter, our advocate on record, R.K. Mehta, rang me up and asked me to be in Delhi, as yet another matter had been listed. I left for the Supreme Court along with one Mr Mitra, who was deputy secretary in health department. Reaching Orissa Bhavan around 10 pm, I just rang up our advocate on record and asked him about the bench where the matter had been listed, and I was told it had come before a bench of Justice Venkataramaya and Justice Fazal Ali. I also told him that we need not engage Mr Parasharan, and that the government wanted I should represent this case. I also told him that he need not send the brief but be present in the court half an hour early. Accordingly, I reached the court little earlier on the next day and went through the matter that had been listed. It did not take much time, since I was very conversant with the matter. As soon as the matter was called, the lawyer for the petitioner submitted that in similar matter, the court had issued notice and had granted provisional order of admission. I stood up and submitted in five minutes as to the nature of the case and the impugned judgement of Orissa High Court and urged upon their lordship that ordinarily no provisional admission should be given and there was no special feature in the case. I further urged that the state apprehended that the medical council would withdraw the recognition, since, without the necessary infrastructure to impart education at the postgraduate level, the authority was bound to comply with the same on account of order of the court. The argument advanced by me was appreciated, and though the bench issued notice, it did not grant any provisional admission. Emboldened by such order, I requested the bench for permission to file application for review and recall of earlier orders. The court granted the permission. Mr Verma, the health secretary, was very pleased and, on telephone, requested me to return to Orissa only after filing the necessary applications for review and recall of earlier orders.

In all, there were about 25 such applications. In those days, as government advocate, I was entitled to only Rs 250 per day irrespective of the number of cases I appeared for in a day. When I intimated this fact to Mr Verma, he assured me that necessary order of the law department would be issued in this particular case. I, therefore, drafted about 25 applications with the help of my advocate on record and asked him to file, and stated that I may be intimated one day before the cases are listed. Within two days of my arrival at Cuttack, I received an order from the law department stating that for this case, being a special one, I would be entitled to Rs 250 per day per case. In connection with such cases, I had to appear in the Supreme Court on four–five occasions and had received a sum of Rs 35,000, which was utilised towards the completion of the first floor of our house. When Advocate General Rath got to know about the order, he asked me as to why I communicated with the government directly instead of telling him. I replied that I had never written to the government and, in fact, the health secretary himself was in the Supreme Court and had got the approval of the same. Mr Rath appeared unhappy but didn't tell me anything. By that time my name had already been sent for elevation and was pending with the central government, and as such I also did not interact any further with the Advocate General.

Soon thereafter the medical admission case was listed before the CJI for final hearing. Mr Verma met me and asked me to proceed to Delhi. I intimated Advocate General Rath and left for Delhi and also informed him that I would return only after witnessing the closing ceremony of Asian Games. Just a day after I reached Delhi, I received a telegram from the advocate general which stated: 'Case not likely to be heard. Come immediately.' I was really surprised to receive a telegram since I had already intimated the Advocate General of my plans. I decided that I would not leave Delhi before the conclusion of Asian Games. So, in the evening, I sent a telegram to the legal remembrancer stating, 'Medical admission case down the list. Should I mention next day or go back?' A copy was also sent to secretary of the health department. On the next day, I received the reply from both of them, stating, 'Mention the matter before the court, try to get the matter heard during the week.' On Monday, I mentioned this matter before the CJI, but the order was, 'Wait till Thursday and will see to take up the matter if possible.' The copy of that order was sent to the health secretary and the legal remembrancer. I was enjoying my stay in Orissa Bhavan and spending time with friends and was arranging an entry pass into the stadium to see the closing ceremony. On Thursday, the matter was taken up, but after listening to me for about 15 minutes, the court ordered that the batch of petitions require full dress hearing and as such the matter be taken up after two months. A particular day was fixed for the same. I stayed for one more day in Delhi and made sure to attend the Asian Games closing ceremony at the Jawaharlal Nehru Stadium.

It was in the first week of May 1983 that the Odia newspapers published my name for being elevated as a judge of Orissa High Court. P.C. Mishra was also named alongside me. On the next day, when I reached the court premises, two very senior lawyers met me in the corridor and told me that they were the accused number one and two in the 1979 incident. I just indicted that I would not like to be reminded of that hurtful episode. They then congratulated me, for which I thanked them.

After the notification of my elevation as judge was published in the newspaper, Advocate General Gangadhar Rath organised a grand dinner in my honour in his residence, where about 50–60 lawyer friends were invited. Mr Rath himself was a good host and would never call for a dinner unless he himself was satisfied with the dishes to be served. I still remember he had hosted a dinner in honour of Chief Justice A.N. Ray. The dishes to be chosen were given to the caterer beforehand and for four days we had to taste each dish and certify its merit.

Lawyers are generally of two kinds: those who get involved in a case so much that they feel as if they are clients, and those who think of it as a profession and would honestly discharge their duties to the extent they think it's possible. Mr Rath and Mr Patnaik were of the first category. Amongst the government lawyers, one would find three categories. One, who becomes overzealous and thinks that state should not lose in any case. Second, who thinks and considers honestly as to what should be the approach and accordingly represents the matter before the court. The third category are those who think that they merely represent the government. Majority of the government lawyers belong to third category, they never try to utilise their own knowledge or intelligence in any matter.

Being attached to the office of the advocate general I had the opportunity of handling a large number of cases relating to all branches of law—civil, criminal and constitutional—and also taxation law, which may not have been possible for a private practitioner. That aside, I could also make a name and standing on my own. The habit of coming to court fully prepared helped me achieve proficiency in different branches of law so much so that with that groundwork I could manage with little efforts while deciding cases as a judge, and it became much easier for me to appreciate the submission of the council and dictating judgement in court.

A lawyer's life can be divided into three stages. In the first stage, there is enough time and mind, but not much money for enjoyment. In the second stage, one gets enough money as well as mind, but does not get much time. In the third stage, one has enough money as well as time but no mind to enjoy. In my life before I reached the third stage, I was elevated as judge of the high court. Even after the 1979 debacle on account of Justice R.N. Mishra, I never entertained any animosity or disrespect towards him. On the other hand, the help I had received while he was in the Bar, his compassion, his friendly behaviour and his helpful attitude will never be forgotten by me. When the necessary baby food for my children was not available in the market, it was his small slip to the health store that made it possible for me to procure the baby food. When the construction work of my Kafla house on the ground floor was almost stopped on account of non-availability of cement in the market, he came forward and sent 50 bags of cement from his Tulsipur house, which was still under construction, and I have all long expressed my gratitude to him. Finally, it was on his recommendation that I was elevated as a judge of Orissa High Court.

I had competed 44 years by then, and I remembered what Mr Shastri had predicted years back, that there would be a change in my career at the age of 45. Lo and behold, there was a change in my career—from advocating as a lawyer to decision-making as a judge. Therefore, I called up Mr Shastri and requested him to attend my oath ceremony.

It was the second week of May, when the warrant for our appointment was received by the high court from the president, hardly a couple of days before the court was closing for summer vacation. P.C. Mishra and I, therefore, decided that we would take oath when the court reopened in the last week of June. Earlier in March, Justice R.N. Mishra, the then chief justice of Orissa High Court, had been elevated as a judge of the Supreme Court, and P.K. Mohanty was the acting chief justice. One day, he called both of us and told us we should not wait till the reopening of the court as the all-India seniority was being considered for appointment as chief justice. He asked us to find a suitable day and proceed with our oath-taking.

Thereafter I went about visiting the senior lawyers to seek their blessings for my new journey ahead. I received several letters of congratulation from friends and relatives. My friend, Nilmadhav, who was in Papua New Guinea then, sent me a congratulatory message on a postcard. My friend Bijoy Pal organised a big dinner in his Bakhrabad house for about 100 lawyers. I also visited Mr B.M. Patnaik and spent a very long time reminiscing the old days with him.

1 June 1983, 11 am, was the appointed hour of oath-taking. Thus began a new chapter in my career. In retrospect, I can say that my career spanning 20 years as an advocate was quite satisfactory for me, judged

from any angle, whether in terms of income or in terms of the reputation and recognition I earned. It was not, of course, up to the mark in terms of acquisition of property or saving money.

Before I move on to talk about the next phase of my life as a judge, my club life may be worth mentioning here. When I had joined the office of Mr B.K. Pal way back in 1961, and had plenty of time at my disposal, my friends and I conceived the idea of a 'Saturday Club'. The club was not a registered one, and neither was there was an article of association nor any rules to be followed. It was merely a club for the congregation of friends belonging to different walks of life in the same age group and with similar mindset. There were never any elections for the posts, and those who were chosen continued throughout their life. The president was S.N. Acharya, who was our law teacher in Madhusudan Law College, who used to play tennis with us and later on became a judge of Orissa High Court. He continued as president even after his retirement. The vice president was one S.S. Padhi, a senior police officer. He continued as vice president even after retirement, but became unwell towards the later part of his life. The secretary was the self-appointed and supremely energetic P.K. Mishra. Lastly, I was the treasurer of the club. But the club had neither a bank account nor any treasury.

Amongst the members, we had a number of doctors, namely Dr D.B. Tompe, one of the best cardiologists in the state; Dr Sabyasachi Das, professor of medicine in the SCB Medical College, Cuttack, and supposedly the best physician in the state; S.N. Panda, a famous urologist; Dr N.K. Das, a radiologist; Dr S. Patnaik, the HOD of the Radiology department in SCB Medical College; Dr M.Y. Rahim, a chest physician; Dr G.S. Tripathi, a pathologist stationed in Sambalpur; Dr C.R. Parija of the Biochemistry department in SCB Medical College; Dr Ashok Bose, professor of anatomy.

Amongst the lawyers who were members of the club were myself, my friends D.P. Mahapatra, who also became a judge and retired as a Judge of Supreme Court of India, and Bijoy Pal. We had one architect named S.C. Mahapatra. We had a civil servant by the name of Nilmadhav Mohanty, who was secretary to Government of India, and then left for a UN assignment. We had one engineer, G.C. Mitra, who went to the top of the career and retired as secretary to the Government in the public works department. We had few corporate professionals like P.K. Mishra and S.C. Ghosh. One businessman who had a small automobile spare parts shop on Cantonment Road, and R. Bhowsinka, who had several businesses. We also had a member, Shanker Roy, who, though eminently qualified, was not engaged in any particular work for his living. He, of course, had landed property in his village and was unmarried. In fact, he was the only unmarried member in the club.

There being no fixed place for the club, the front lawn of my bungalow on 6, Cantonment Road was utilised as the club premise. Before my elevation as a judge, Supreme Motors (my friend Bablu's shop) was the venue. Spending Saturday evenings together over dinner and discussion on a variety of subjects, except politics, was our main activity. Our spouses were not invited to most of these congregations, but we'd also have dinner nights with the spouses and sometimes a family picnic. A visit to Madhupur House on Puri sea beach on 14th August night and to Konark for celebrating 26 January, more particularly on the midnight of 25th January, were almost an annual affair.

Visiting Calcutta during December to watch the test match and spending New Years' eve in Park Street was yet another annual feature. The arrangement of rooms in Utkal Bhawan in Calcutta and arranging tickets for going to cricket matches were my responsibilities. Mr Kailash

Chandra Das, who was an employee of Orissa Olympic Association, and Barrister Ranjit Mohanty helped us for several years in arranging the required number of tickets. While returning to Utkal Bhawan after a whole day at Eden Gardens, a masseur was engaged for us, and this was arranged by Shankar Roy. On several occasions, after dinner at Trincas in Park Street, while returning to Utkal Bhavan on Wellington Square, we went to Saki Bar on Dharamtala Street not to have a drink but only to experience the nighttime scene at the bar. We even went on road trips to places such as Delhi, Agra, Madras, Bangalore, Mumbai, Jamshedpur, Vizag and Koraput.

Most of the club members have already left this world today, and the so-called family get-togethers organised annually in the high court guest house on Cantonment Road has been abandoned since 2020. Nowadays we stay in touch on telephone and try to ask after each other's well-being whenever we can.

# Judge at Orissa High Court

The day I was sworn in as a judge of Orissa High Court, 1 June 1983, remains etched as an important and memorable day in my life. Since 10 am was the time fixed for administering the oath, I got up early that morning and after taking a bath went to the Cuttack Chandi Temple to offer my prayers. It was on the insistence of Loka Nana, the head priest at the local temple that I visited often; he passed away recently. It took me about half an hour at the temple, and when I came back home, my father suddenly asked me as to whether I had met Barrister Ranjit Mohanty. I answered that I did not feel like meeting him hence I had not visited him. My father almost commanded me to visit him before leaving for the high court. I could hardly disobey my father's command, and reluctantly made my way to Barrister Mohanty's house, which was close to ours.

When I reached his house, I found him on the first floor talking to his wife. Surprisingly, upon seeing me, a strapping man like him stood up and started weeping. I felt embarrassed. I apologised to him for not being able to visit him earlier to pay my respects and to seek his blessings, and informed him that I would have to leave early to be able to make it to the oath ceremony on time. He didn't leave me until I took a sweet from his hand. When I returned home, my father told me that since Mr Mohanty was a senior member in the profession, his blessings would help me in the future, even though he was aware of Mr Mohanty's role in leading the campaign against me in 1979. It is then that I realised what my father meant, which speaks a lot about the attitude of the people in those days.

Justice J.K. Mohanty had told me that he would pick me up on his way to the high court for my oath-taking ceremony. So, I had sent my wife and children in my car earlier. Although I had requested my father to come to court, he didn't agree. Justice Mohanty reached on time, and I left with him in his car. On the portico, the registrar of court welcomed me with a flower bouquet. My *jamadaar*, who was also there, took me to my chamber, which was a small one. There, I put on my robes and left for the chamber of the chief justice, where brother judges had already gathered. There were only five judges then, including the acting chief justice. After a short while, CM J.B. Patnaik arrived, followed by the governor of Orissa.

The oath-taking ceremony of a high court judge used to be performed with much pomp and grandeur as compared to the oath-taking ceremony of a judge at the Supreme Court. In a procession, the governor, the acting chief justice, the two judges-designate and the registrar left the chambers for the conference hall. The procession was led by several employees bearing different insignia of the high court. By the time we reached the conference hall, I was surprised to find it almost full, even though the court was officially closed for summer vacation. Guests included the cabinet minister and members of the Bar. As far as personal guests were concerned, my wife and children, and my cousin and his wife were the only relations of mine present, whereas my colleague P.C. Mishra had a large number of his relations in attendance. Few friends of mine had also made it to the ceremony, such as the then Finance Secretary Mr Bhujabal, the then Secretary Irrigation Mr Hota, and Mr Shankar Roy from the Saturday Club. Justice R.N. Mishra, who was then a judge of Supreme Court and was in Cuttack on account of summer vacation, was also present at the ceremony.

After the oath ceremony, there was a small high-tea for the guests that lasted for about an hour. I left the event with Justice J.K. Mohanty and, on the way, dropped in to meet retired Justice R.K. Das in his house at Dagarpara. There, I found the CM present, and given the opportunity, requested him for the allotment of an official bungalow, as my Kafla house was not big enough to house the staff, which included a secretary, a personal assistant and a few household helps that I would have to maintain as a judge. The CM promised that he would look into the matter and expressed his regret for the delay of four years in my appointment, as he was well aware of what went on in 1979. Within six days, the deputy secretary to the Orissa government in the general administration department reached my house with an order of allotment of the bungalow on 6, Cantonment Road in my name.

Orissa High Court reopened on 16 June 1983, and I was sitting in division bench with Acting Chief Justice P.K. Mohanty. That day, when I touched my father's feet before leaving for court, my father expressed his sorrow at the absence of my mother, who could not see me as a judge of the high court. Then he gave me a word of caution and stated that even though the Almighty had conferred immense power on me as a judge of the high court, I should not misuse the same, particularly against those who had stood in the way of my appointment back in 1979. As such, I continued as a judge of Orissa High Court for 13 long years, and many of those lawyers appeared before me in several cases, but I never held any grudge against them nor passed any adverse order merely on that score. My father's words of caution stayed with me throughout my career as a judge.

The new phase of life as a judge brought with it many changes. In place of being a public prosecutor and a defender of the orders of the executive government, I became an adjudicator to decide the lis mostly between the state and litigant public. Income reduced and expenses increased. In those days, the salary of a high court judge was Rs 3,500 per month, and no dearness allowance was admissible. A judge had to pay a percentage of his salary towards the government bungalow, charges for electricity and even the petrol for his own car. Again, a judge was required to lead a somewhat restricted life. Even then, in my opinion, on the whole, the life of a judge was more peaceful and without any hazards, and, in a way, quite enjoyable. Many of my friends after being elevated as a judge usually complain the sacrifices they have had to make by giving up the lucrative practice at the Bar. I always argue with them that becoming a judge is more about prestige and not about the money, as one can always refuse an appointment. I remember many a colleague who had tried to become a judge, but not having been successful at the right time, had refused when offered at a much later time.

One instance comes to mind. In 1966, the then chief justice of Orissa High Court had recommended the name of Barrister B.M Patnaik for elevation as judge. The government did not agree, and as a result the proposal could not go through. Then in 1978, when he was again offered the judgeship, he refused. Similarly, when Justice G.K. Mishra was the chief justice, he had recommended the name of Barrister Rajit Mohanty for elevation. At that point of time, he was chairman of the Bar Council of India and he made some adverse comment against the PM of India for which the proposal did not succeed, and when later he was offered again, naturally he refused.

In the meanwhile, I visited the 6, Cantonment Road bungalow with my wife to find out what immediate repair work would be necessary before we could move in to the bungalow. By that time the construction of the ring road on the riverbank was in full swing, and as such fixing of grilles on the open verandah of the bungalow was a necessity from a security point of view. The executive engineer who was present, upon query, stated that the job would require at least Rs 60,000, which would need to be sanctioned from the government. The director of the estates, who was also present there, stated that he had already initiated the process. As we were keen to move early, I visited the bungalow from time to time to check on the repair work, and to my surprise, found that no work had been done. Fed up with the situation, I rang up my friend, who was the Finance Secretary, and arranged a meeting with the director of the estate and the engineer concerned at the bungalow on a Sunday. When my friend arrived for the meeting, the engineer suddenly sprang to action and came up with a list of additional renovations that needed to be done. In the course of discussion, my friend observed in passing that the if work is completed within two weeks, he would ensure that whatever finance was necessary he would get it sanctioned. After that, the work started immediately and was completed within 15 days. But by the end of it, although the estimated expenses came to be two–three times more than what I was given to understand on the first occasion, the said money was sanctioned by the finance department. It was later that I learnt from my friend, much to my embarrassment, that there was much to and fro between departments before he could get the renovation expenses sanctioned. I stayed in that house for more than 12 years, but never requested any further alteration in the bungalow. After I left Orissa, I was told that many judges renovated their government bungalows at the expense of the public exchequer, and I was really surprised to find that the government was also sanctioning the amount. I have all along thought that a government bungalow allotted to a judge is nothing but a guest house, and therefore, it is futile to make any unnecessary expense on account of its renovation.

We performed a small housewarming pooja in our house in September and shifted one or two days thereafter. The bungalow was a huge one with a big living room, a big dining room, four bedrooms with attached bathrooms, a kitchen, a storeroom and a very big office room, with a room for a private secretary and a bathroom attached to same. There was a huge courtyard, which housed the staff quarters. What a change for us—from a single room in our Kafla house to individual bedrooms for each of our children. I had a great desire to bring my father with me, but he never agreed. He walked down to our bungalow at least once every week but never stayed overnight. However, I made sure that my car would drop him back home.

The front portion of the bungalow was developed as a sprawling lawn. Those days, there used to be a competition to find out the best garden in the town, and every year our garden was adjudged the best. The credit, of course, goes to Bijoy Ram Das, who was a soil conservationist but had the sense to give a layout for the garden and select the appropriate plants to be planted all around. It was so planned that one would find flowers throughout the year. The beautiful creeper on the roof of the house used to give a very grand look from a distance.

During this phase of my life, not only did my role in the court change, but several old habits came to an end and new ones were formed. Lunch around 1:30 pm became the new norm. Catching up with friends at Supreme Motors stopped. Our house was referred as the bungalow, and our domestic help used to address us as Sahib and Memsahib, which my wife never liked but could not change.

Back at the high court, even though ordinarily newly appointed judges did not participate in any case discussions, I participated in almost all cases discussions from the very beginning. In fact, any discussion by me on question of law as well as on the fact of that particular case was even encouraged by Acting Chief Justice P.K. Mohanty. I did not find difficulty in participating when the case was being heard, but the most difficult part was sitting for long hours in the courtroom. A lawyer, while arguing, never sits on a chair, and then a busy lawyer moves from one court to the other, but a judge is forced to sit on the chair right from the beginning till the end, with only a single break in between. It took me about two weeks to get accustomed to this new habit. At the end of the week, the acting chief justice passed on two cases to me that were reserved for delivery of judgement for writing the judgement, with a word of caution stating that since this would be my first judgement in life, I must devote much time and think over the matter before dictating the judgement. I completed those two judgements within a week and sent the draft for approval to the acting chief justice. He took the trouble of going through both the judgements very minutely and then called me to intimate that the judgements were much above the standard he had expected and needed no correction, and directed the registry to put up those two judgements for delivery in court the following day. Not only did he convey his appreciation by telephoning me but he also went on to mention the same before the brother judges, so much that on the next day, before I left my chambers for home at 4:30 pm, two brother judges wanted the copy of judgement just to read. This very attitude of the acting chief justice encouraged me to a great extent.

The acting chief justice became so very confident of my ability that very soon he constituted a single judge bench for me and also told me that he would ask the registry to list different types of cases for me, mostly civil. The same evening, I found that the cases were civil revisions, miscellaneous appeals and second appeals. I had made up my mind that as far as possible I would deliver judgement in court after hearing counsel for the party. I, therefore, asked my private secretary and my personal assistant both to be present in court so that it would be easier for me to dictate the judgement alternately to them. I read the brief of at least the first 10 cases in the list to facilitate the delivery of judgement in court. As per my plan, I heard eight cases, two miscellaneous appeals, two second appeals and four civil revisions, and dictated judgement in all the cases in court. As I was prepared, having read the briefs beforehand, I did not have any difficulty in dictating judgement in court. I kept this habit throughout my career as a judge unless, of course, a case required much deliberation for dictating the judgement. I always preferred to deliver the judgement in court. According to me, two benefits are derived in the process. Firstly, since the judgement is being dictated in the presence of lawyers of both the sides, the possibility of committing any error on facts disappears and, secondly, you do not have any backlog requiring additional work on weekends.

Justice P.K. Mohanty continued as acting chief justice till Justice D. Pathak from Guwahati High Court was appointed as chief justice of Orissa High Court. Thereafter, Justice Mohanty continued as puisne judge and ultimately retired as a judge of Orissa High Court. In my opinion, gross injustice was done by not making him a permanent chief justice of a high court. Under our constitutional scheme, the appointment of a judge to the high court as well as its chief justice is governed by Article 217. Ever since 1950, a judge of the high court as well as its chief justice were being appointed by president of India in consultation with the CJI and the governor of the state. It was also the convention and practice that the senior-most judge of a high court was appointed as the Chief Justice of the high court. After about 30–35 years, in a conference of the chief justices of the high court and the CMs of states, a decision was taken that the chief justices of a high court should not be from the same court. The thinking amongst the Bar members was that a judge by virtue of his continued stay in a state develops bias and is likely to show favouritism to chosen few, and therefore, it would be better to have a chief justice from outside the state. In the event, it was also the understanding that the senior-most judge of a particular high court should be appointed as a chief justice of some other high court. In other words, the right of the senior-most judge of a high court should not be affected in any manner. Under the aforesaid scenario, when the permanent chief justice of Orissa High Court, R.N. Mishra, was elevated as a judge of the Supreme Court sometime in March 1983, and when the president decided to appoint Justice D. Pathak of Guwahati High Court as chief justice of Orissa High Court, in all fairness, Justice P.K. Mohanty should have been appointed as chief justice of some other high court, but that was not the case.

That apart, a practice had developed by which two or three persons from a particular high court were being appointed as chief justices of three different high courts at one point of time, whereas the senior-most judges of several high courts were overlooked. From my own experience, I am of the view that small high courts and the judges of those high courts were being overlooked in the matter of being appointed as a chief justice of a high court or as a judge of the Supreme Court. Or else there could not have been any justifiable reason as to why after the first appointment from Orissa High Court to the Supreme Court was made in 1952 when Bachu Jagannath Das was elevated, it took another 31 years for Justice R.N. Mishra from Orissa to be appointed to the Supreme Court in March 1983. Many suitable persons from Orissa High Court, who were undoubtedly competent, were overlooked in the consideration for elevation to the Supreme Court, such as B.K. Ray, the first chief justice of the court, Justice S.P. Mahapatra, Chief Justice G.K. Mishra and Dr B.N. Mishra, to name a few. The power for appointment to the high court and Supreme Court was taken over by the Supreme Court through a body called 'collegium' not by the amendment of the Constitution but by a process of interpreting a particular provision of the Constitution conferring the primacy on the opinion of the CJI in the consultative process, as reflected in the Advocate of Record Association Case, 1993 (4 SCC page 441).

In this context, I remember as a young judge, when the CJI R.S. Pathak was visiting Orissa, a tea party had been organised, and in that party, the CJI enquired as to what were the grievances of the judges of the court. There were about eight-nine judges by then in Orissa High Court, and I was still the youngest. Nobody put any question to the CJI, but I did raise my hand and, on being allowed, I asked one question—namely how was it that at a given point of time there could be three persons from one high court being appointed as chief justices of different high courts, while there could be none from some high courts. The CJI probably did not anticipate this question, and he called me to his side and answered, with his hand over my shoulder, 'Young man, there is something called court management; you will know in course of time.' I was not satisfied with the answer on that day nor am I satisfied with it even today. Since the Constitution never contemplated a situation like this and, by taking advantage of a decision arrived at in the joint meeting of the chief justices of high courts and the CMs, the competent authority, be it the executive government prior to the Second Judges Case in 1993 or the collegium substituting thereafter, the practice of bestowing favour on a few persons at the cost of denying the rights of some other persons continued. It was a case of mere pick and choose by the appointing authority without any rationale.

Justice D. Pathak, who took over as chief justice of Orissa High Court was no doubt a gentleman but lacked sincerity. He did little to find out the loopholes in the so-called delay in disposal of cases or finding a solution to the problem. During his tenure, once he had given instruction to the registrar to issue a circular to the bench clerk of each of the judges to note down the time when the judge sits in the court and when he gets up, and submit the same to the chief justice by the evening. He was probably trying to keep a control on the functioning of the individual judges. On a particular day, after the implementation of that circular, when I was about to rise 10 minutes before the schedule time, my bench clerk informed me about the said circular, but I did not listen. Coming back to my chamber, I felt really humiliated, since I thought it would have been prudent for the chief justice to at least inform each of the judges about the circular. In the event, my brother judges and I took up the matter with the chief justice at his residence, and I remember to have told the learned chief justice then that a court functions as a team, and it should be the effort of the chief justice as the *karta* of a coparcenary to take every judge with him rather than trying to control them. The chief justice, however, had revoked the circular by then, having been alerted beforehand by a brother judge form our group, and the evening ended in tea and sweets. Thereafter, the chief justice never tried any such measures during his tenure.

It is during the tenure of Chief Justice Pathak that my brother-in-law got married in April 1984. He married the eldest daughter of Anil Bihari Das, an advocate of Angul, and her name was Sanghamitra. Anil Bihari was the son of Gagan Bihari Das, the most well-known lawyer of Angul. My brother-in-law then was serving with Escorts after his MBA degree from XLRI, Jamshedpur. Since my parents-in law were no longer alive, I was hosting his wedding. I organised a party before the date of marriage and most of the judges, including the chief justice, attended the same. Majority of the judges of Orissa High Court had accompanied the procession to Angul and the reception was organised at our bungalow at 6, Cantonment Road. My father was quite active then and not only was he present all through the marriage ceremony but also actively supervised the reception ceremony that was held two days after. But on the date of marriage a sudden outburst of rains disturbed the programme, and we could not start before 6 pm. The storm and rain that evening became stumbling block as the space within our compound became muddy. In those days, it was a sit down dinner, and the guests would be served batch after batch. When I became worried and was thinking of an alternative venue, Mr B.R. Das, the OMP Commandant, assured me venue will be fully ready in one day and I should not worry. He also told me even the police people would serve the food. I had requested the governor to provide the band and that was immediately approved. I did not invite the governor or the CM to avoid any chaos. The reception ceremony went on smoothly and also was to the great satisfaction of my wife, who was the head of their family.

During the tenure of Justice Pathak, Justice J.K. Mohanty, the senior-most judge, was appointed as chief justice of Sikkim High Court. He had been in Sikkim for more than two years, and on his request and insistence, I planned a visit to Gangtok with my second son and daughter once and spent a pleasant week with him. Even though I was declared as State Guest, he insisted that we should stay in his quarters and not in the State Guest House. We visited not only Nathu La pass, the border between India and China, but also several parts of Sikkim. Both Justice Mohanty and his wife were wonderful hosts, and I still remember the personal attention and the hospitality we received there.

During those days, a high court judge was entitled to leave travel concession (LTC) privilege once every two years, which included journey by train in AC 2-tier to any destination, but it should be from point to point. So, I had planned a trip to South India with my family during the puja vacation, when court would remain closed for about two weeks. Our first stop was Madras, or Chennai, as it is now known. We were hosted as State Guest by the Tamil Nadu government, so accommodation was arranged in the State Guest House in Madras. From there, we had planned a visit to the famous Tirupati temple. Accommodation had been arranged in the guest house of the temple, but the best part was the darshan of

Lord Tirupati and the gift of a dozen ladoos from the temple committee. While the waiting time for normal *darshan* was around two hours, we were fortunate to have been escorted to the main temple chamber right away and experience *darshan* of the deity for more than 20 minutes with a special *aarti*. At that moment, I realised what great privilege came with the position of a judge. Even today, after retirement, the same privileges are available to me and my family all over the country, and I am grateful for all the respect I receive.

Our family then proceeded to Bangalore, where we spent a couple of days visiting various tourist sites. From there we went to Mysore with the hope of witnessing the Dusshera celebrations. However, we had to leave abruptly anticipating the rush in the event of the President's visit during the same time. We then proceeded to Ooty in Tamil Nadu via Bandipore Reserve Forest. On being intimated about our desire to spend one night at Bandipore, the district judge of Mysore obliged us by getting us accommodation for the night at the Bandipore Reserve Forest.

The stay at Bandipore was quite an unique experience. The forest officer had told us not to come out of the cottage during the night and not to be scared if elephants came knocking on the door. True to his word, around 11 pm, a tusker reached the cottage and started pulling out some branches of the tree adjacent to the cottage. We quietly watched through the window. Early morning next day, around 6:30 am, I got up and opened the door of the cottage to find at least 200 deers moving around the cottage like a flock of sheep. After breakfast, we moved to Ooty, where we spent the time visiting the old British bakeries and enjoying the pleasant mountain weather.

After three days, we came back to Bangalore by car and left for Belgaum by train where my wife's cousin was staying and her husband, who was employed with Indian Aluminium. While at Belgaum, he suggested that we can visit Goa by car for two nights. Even though Goa was not within our LTC plan, since we had not seen the place earlier, we lapped up the opportunity and left for Goa in his Ambassador. I had sent an intimation to the Goa bench of Bombay High Court, and they arranged accommodation for us in the circuit house. Spending two nights at Goa, we returned to Belgaum, and from there proceeded to Hubli to catch the train for Secunderabad. At Secunderabad, a young police officer, who was the brother of advocate Ashok Mohanty, was there to receive us, but we did not have time and so we proceeded straight to the railway station to catch the train which was coming from Bombay and proceeding to Bhubaneshwar. Mr Mohanty, however, gave us so much food that it became sufficient not only for our lunch but also for our dinner during our journey to Bhubaneswar. The train had only Third Class compartment, and we had one full block consisting of four berths reserved for us, and there were eight police constables who came with us and they did not allow the seats on either side of our block to be occupied by anybody. They came right up to Berhampur in Orissa. That was an extra arrangement made by Andhra Police, thanks to Mr Mohanty. This is how the first LTC of my service career was availed.

When the service condition of judges got changed and rules were amended, LTC facility was made available twice every year with the provision of travel in AC First Class or by air in Business Class. Later on, when I moved to the Supreme Court, it became thrice a year. I utilised the perk every year, and that made it possible for me to visit every nook and corner of interest in the country, right from Kashmir to Kanyakumari. If you are treated as State Guest, then you do not have to pay neither for your stay or food or transport, and the only thing you have to pay for is your own shopping. Such were the perks associated with the legal profession I had reluctantly taken up in my youth!

On the retirement of Justice Pathak, Dr Justice B.N. Mishra was appointed the acting chief justice. During this time, the entire judiciary of the state underwent a massive rehaul. Every presiding judge of every court in every part of the state started coming to court on time. Even the high court building had a different look, and promptness and cleanliness became the standard. Surprise court inspections became a regular thing. The officer of the registry was changed, and even the constitution of standing committee was altered. Justice Mishra brought in judges on whom he had confidence and trust to the standing committee. But his tenure was quite short-lived, and then came in Justice H.L. Aggarwal, the senior-most judge from Patna High Court, as the chief justice of Orissa High Court.

I knew Justice Aggarwal from a brief encounter during my trip to Tirupati and Mysore. He was a religious man and used to visit Lord Jagannath at Puri almost every month during his tenure. Few months thereafter, Dr Justice B.N. Mishra was transferred to Allahabad High Court as puisne judge. The members of the Bar felt that his transfer was done at the behest of a judge of Orissa who was then in the Supreme Court. In the event, the Bar decided to go on strike, which continued for more than three weeks without yielding any result. Dr Justice B.N. Mishra, however, accepted the transfer without much protest, and most of us were surprised at such a turn of events. The rumour was that the son of the learned judge from Orissa, who was then in the Supreme Court, was practising as an advocate in Orissa High Court and did not get any special favour from Dr Justice Mishra, for which he was transferred.

Two incidents during the tenure of Chief Justice Aggarwal are worth mentioning here. On receipt of certain irregularity committed by one district judge, Justice Aggarwal himself enquired into the matter and found him to have committed the irregularity and suggested that the district judge concerned should not be given selection grade. The power of punishing a district judge vests with the high court, namely the full court and not with the chief justice alone. So, the enquiry report together with the recommendation needed approval of full court. When the matter came up for discussion in the full court meeting, the report given to the judges was quite bulky. I was then the third senior-most judge in Orissa High Court by then, and I was surprised that out of eight–nine judges, nobody raised any objection to considering the report in that meeting. But I raised the objection that since the report had not been given to the judges earlier, without going through the same, it would not be possible to express an opinion. Some judges did observe that since the chief justice himself had enquired into the matter, the question of its consideration did not arise. I, however, strongly protested on the ground that an enquiry report against the senior-most district judge in the cadre, constituting about 25–30 pages, cannot be taken up for consideration without going through the same. Chief Justice Aggarwal was displeased with my comment and observed that hence forward he would not like to hold any enquiry. I also politely replied that whether the chief justice would like to go on enquiry or not was his personal choice, but under law, a report has to be accepted by full court, and such acceptance could only be given only after going through the report. The agenda in the meeting, therefore, was adjourned. But, surprisingly, just three days thereafter, when I had gone to Allahabad in connection with the immersion of my father's ashes at Sangam, a full court meeting was convened, and the decision was taken to not allow the district judge selection grade, which was otherwise due to him. He filed a review petition, and when that petition was taken up in the next full court meeting, I was present but was not participating. I did not want to express views on the matter since the decision had been taken purposely at a point of time when I was absent from Cuttack. Consequently, the said district judge filed a writ petition challenging the administrative order of the full court and the matter came up before me along with the Justice Mrs A.K. Padhi, and the administrative decision was quashed, and he was granted relief of super time scale. Within a year of that happening, he was elevated as a judge of the high court. Having gone through the enquiry report conducted by the chief justice, I suspected that the chief justice was made to enquire at the behest of two other judges of the high court who were also service judges and might have held a grudge against the district judge who, as a result, was punished in the report of Justice Aggarwal. Such things do happen and can only be considered as a service hazard.

The other instance during the tenure of Chief Justice Aggarwal was with regard his recommendation of the name of one member of the High Court Bar for elevation as a judge of the high court. The said gentleman was basically a tax practitioner but the file did not move in the office of the CM for a pretty long time and the reason was that the CM had told the chief justice that the case of a senior-most member in the cadre of district judge should be considered and be sent for elevation. The chief justice was adamant not to send his name, the ground being the said senior-most district judge had become a member of the Orissa State Administrative Tribunal and as such was ineligible. The lawyer from the Bar whose name had been recommended by the chief justice met me in my chamber during lunch hour one day and requested me to make a request to the CM for movement of his file to the central government. I was reluctant, but relented upon his insistence and fixed up an appointment with the CM at his residence. During my meeting with the CM, upon my query as to why he was insisting on the elevation of the senior-most district judge, the answer was candid. He said that the senior-most district judge was his roommate in the hostel when they were pursuing their graduation course in Ravenshaw College, and that he being the senior-most judge in the cadre and his confidential character roll being outstanding there was no reason why his case should not be considered. I quite appreciated the frankness of the CM and did not press the matter any further.

The next day, when the said lawyer met me in my chamber, I narrated the entire conversation with the CM and told him that his file would not move until the chief justice changed his mind. The lawyer then requested me to report the same to the chief justice. I frankly told him that I was not that friendly with the chief justice and my approaching him on the matter might be considered interference with his powers. But the lawyer kept pestering me, and so I told him that I would meet the chief justice.

The very same day, after court hours, I met the Chief Justice Aggarwal in his chamber and apprised him of what transpired between me and the CM. He, however, told me that since he had not seen the senior-most district judge of the cadre, it was not possible for him to recommend his case. I replied that recommendation of a district judge was made on the basis of the confidential character roll, and full court of Orissa High Court had given him 'outstanding' for last few years. The other consideration was the impeccable reputation of the person. Nevertheless, the chief justice was quite adamant and told me that he would not recommend the said senior-most district judge. I left his chamber having told him that the recommendation made by him would not move the precincts of the office of CM until and unless the case of the senior-most district judge was received in the office of CM.

I do not know what happened that night, but on the next day, Chief Justice Aggarwal met me and told that he had had a chance to think over the matter and had finally sent the proposal for elevation of the senior-most district judge as desired by the CM. Ultimately, both of them were appointed as judges of Orissa High Court on the same day and became my learned colleagues on the bench. Years later, when Chief Justice H.L. Aggarwal had retired and was practising as a lawyer in the Supreme Court, he reached out to me to arrange for his accommodation in Orissa. I had then reminded him that his disciple, whom he had recommended for elevation as judge, was the acting chief justice of Orissa and could also be approached for the same. But the answer I received was really painful, for he said that he had been trying to contact the acting chief justice but was not able to get him on phone. I was really surprised and shocked at this answer and thought to myself how quickly the said person forgot the help rendered to him, without which he could not have been on the chair he was occupying. I had then replied to Mr Aggrawal that probably his disciple was not thinking that he would also retire one day.

When I became a judge in June 1983, I thought of starting the construction of a house on the land I had purchased in Bhubaneswar while I was an advocate. I made an application for a house loan, and as per the rules prevalent then, the government sanctioned only Rs 75,000. After sometime, the rules got amended, and the amount of loan for house building was enhanced to Rs 2,50,000. I then asked the finance secretary as to whether I would be entitled to avail myself of the same enhanced amount, and he replied that the rule was meant for those who made an application thereafter, but, nevertheless, he asked me to send a letter of request and he would see to the matter. I made an application on the very same day, and to my pleasant surprise, received an order of the finance department within a couple of days sanctioning an additional sum of Rs 1,75,000 as house building advance. When I received the extra loan amount, I decided to visit Europe by spending a part of the same in purchasing air tickets to London. From my childhood, I held a cherished desire to visit the city of London. When I was a school student, a relation of mine had read my palm and told me that there was no foreign trip in my fate line. In 1961–62, when I chose the legal profession as my career, I realised that the dream of going abroad to see the city of London would remain unfulfilled, since there would be no occasion for a lawyer to go aboard. In the meanwhile, Ira, the younger sister of my wife, was settled in Birmingham, UK, with her husband. They were all along requesting us to visit them, but I was not able to arrange the necessary funds for the same. Thus, when I received the advance, I decided it was about time I planned my trip to London. We quickly applied for our Visa and received them well in time. Without any delay, I contacted my travel agent and requested him for two tickets. Within a weeks' time, he met me at my residence and handed me two tickets in economy class by British Airways (Delhi–London and back). In addition, the tickets also enabled us to visit Zurich in Switzerland. He also gave me air tickets from Bhubaneswar to Delhi and back. The entire expense came to about Rs 40,000. During those days, a tourist was allowed to carry only 500 dollars, so I asked Mr Aggarwal to get me 1,000 dollars for which I had to pay Rs 13000 in Indian currency. A friend of mine, an architect, who had returned from the USA had given me a cheque of 500 dollars. So, with 1,500 dollars in hand, my wife and I left for our trip to Europe sometime in June during summer vacation. We covered England, Scotland, Switzerland, Germany and France. Of course, our stay in different places had been arranged with our relatives or any friends, and only in London we stayed in a hotel for four nights.

When I got down at London and was proceeding towards the exit, I thought to myself how people from England had ruled us for so many years and how in our childhood we used to get frightened seeing an Englishman on the sea beach at Puri. We were received at the airport by my sister-in-law and her husband, I just smiled and thought within myself that it was because of them that it was possible for us to visit the UK and incidentally other places in Europe. We visited Scotland with them by car and met a doctor friend who was then a consultant in Glasgow. Scotland was undoubtedly very scenic, and the city of Edinburgh was one of the nicest cities I saw then. Taking a flight from

London to Zurich, we stayed with our niece, whose husband took us to key places like Interlaken, Geneva and Luzern by car, and each of those places had its own charm. Finally, we boarded a train and got down at Dusseldorf in Germany. We stayed with a young engineer there, who was from Cuttack. He took us around a few places in Germany and also took us to Amsterdam in Holland by car. With him we could visit East Berlin also, which was then under communist rule, and were accompanied by Professor Jayant Mahapatra, a well-known English poet, who incidentally was my physics teacher during my intermediate days. From there, we went to Paris by train, where we spent three days. Finally, we came back to London by flight and took a bus ride to Leicester, where my sister-in-law was staying. Even though I was keen on spending some more time in Europe, but since Chief Justice Aggarwal was to retire and had requested me to come back, I did not extend my stay and came back to India as per schedule. My visit to Europe left an indelible imprint on my mind.

After the retirement of Justice Aggarwal and pending the appointment of the permanent chief justice, the senior-most judge in Orissa High Court, R.C. Patnaik, was appointed the acting chief justice. During this time, one incident that I remember needs mention. I was sitting with acting chief justice Patnaik in his chamber when another brother judge entered and questioned him as to why a case that was heard by him in part had been withdrawn from his list and by whose order. The answer the acting chief justice gave was that the listing of the case is always under the order of the chief justice, and so obviously it was under his order that the part heard case had been withdrawn from the list, the reason being that the lawyer who was arguing before him in the case was helping him with purchasing some land in Cuttack, and since that had been brought to his notice, it was only for his benefit that he had withdrawn the case. The learned judge then walked out of his chamber in anger.

Few months thereafter, Justice B.L. Hansaria from Guwahati High Court was appointed as the chief justice of Orissa High Court. It was during his tenure that the judges began meeting over tea every Friday afternoon. He also hosted parties frequently at his official residence for the judges and their spouses, and participated in playing Holi with us every year. In a way, he was very friendly with the judges of the court. As a chief justice, Justice Hansaria was reluctant to go on tour to different district headquarters, even though on several occasions in full court meetings, we had requested him to do so. I think on one occasion I reminded him that as the chief justice of the high court, it was his primary responsibility to see to the smooth functioning of the judiciary within the state. Somehow, initially, he didn't pay any attention in that regard. But later on, he started visiting the different district headquarters. In every full court meeting, Chief Justice Hansaria used to impress upon us that Orissa should follow the Guwahati precedence and model. Initially nobody reacted, but after four–five such instances, in one full court meeting, when he broached the subject of amendment of the rule for introducing the Guwahati model, I politely stated that each high court has its own tradition. The rules and tradition which were being followed by Orissa High Court were brought in from Patna High Court, though there had been some modifications also. As such, I thought there was no need for introducing the Guwahati model unless the entire court felt that it would improve the present system. He appreciated the same and thereafter never mentioned the Guwahati model as long as he continued as chief justice of Orissa High Court. My idea of objecting to his proposal was in view of the scenario which was then prevalent with the chief justice being appointed from different high courts. If every chief justice would start implementing the model of the high court from which they had come, it would be a recipe for disaster.

During his tenure, a case I dealt with deserves mention here. The then CM of Orissa, Mr Biju Patnaik, had made a public speech which was quite derogatory towards the judiciary, stating that 'the high court judges are only white elephants.' In the event, The chief justice himself, sitting with some other judge issued notice of contempt, but when that matter got matured for hearing, he himself was not prepared to take it up and called me to his chamber. He told me that no other judge was coming forward to take up the matter against the CM and requested me to take up the case sitting with Justice P.C. Mishra, who had also taken oath as judge on the same day I had taken oath but was older than me by almost half a decade. We took up the case for hearing, and Justice Mishra wrote the judgement dropping the contempt proceeding following the principle enunciated by Supreme Court in the Shiv Shankar matter, 1988 (3 SCC page 167). Shiv Shankar, as Union law minister had made some derogatory remark, but ultimately the Supreme Court dropped the proceedings. When I went through the draft judgement sent by brother P.C. Mishra, while I agreed with the conclusion of dropping the contempt proceedings, I had given a separate judgement expressing disapproval of the words used by CM. I had observed that the administration of justice and the judges of superior courts may be open to public criticism or public scrutiny, but a criticism of the system or the judges by such a high office as the CM must be prevented. Although criticism of the judicial system or judges should be welcomed so long as such criticism does not impair or hamper the administration of justice and so long as the said criticism does not amount to ridiculing the system. As part of the judgement, I observed that the speech of the CM, which said that there is no justice for poor and that the Rs 2.5 lakh being spent for the upkeep of each judge is like maintaining a white elephant, cannot but be seen in any other light than intemperate language and is not expected from a person holding the high office of the CM of the state. When the judgement was delivered, the CM was very keen to move the Supreme Court for expunction of comments made by me, but ultimately his legal advisor prevailed upon him not to move the Supreme Court, since there was a greater danger of getting further adverse comments, and finally, he dropped the idea.

It was during the tenure of Chief Justice Hansaria that the senior-most puisne judge R.C. Patnaik was elevated as a judge of the Supreme Court. The CJI then was Justice R.N. Mishra from Orissa High Court, and Justice Patnaik was his junior in his office when Justice Mishra was practising in the high court. In all-India seniority list, the position of Judge Patnaik was 58 or 59, and thus on his elevation, he superseded the claim of 57 persons, which was undoubtedly unjust. That apart, I learnt from other sources that few months prior to retirement, Justice Mishra had met the PM, and the latter had asked him as to what he would like to get from the government. The reply had been that he would like to fill up a vacancy in the Supreme Court cadre that would arise on his eventual retirement, and the PM had readily agreed. In the event, Justice Mishra had lost no time to send the name of Justice Patnaik, which was accepted by the government, and he took oath after the retirement of Justice Mishra.

When I started my practice in 1962, allegations of corruption were being heard against one or two magistrates and one subordinate judge in the whole state of Orissa. And even after 22 years of my practice, when I took oath as a judge of Orissa High Court, corruption cases were still being heard against one or two judges of the high court. And again after 13 years, by the time I took oath as a Judge of the Supreme Court, allegations of corruption against some of the judges of every high court were being heard. And while I was continuing as a judge of Supreme Court. Allegation of corruption had been heard against one or two judges of the Supreme Court. In fact, after my retirement in one case, in a contempt proceeding against Advocate Prashant Bhushan, his father Mr Shanti Bhushan, who was the law minister of India in PM Morarji Desai's cabinet, a senior advocate filed an affidavit making a statement that he had information that at least eight of the former CJIs were corrupt. After this affidavit was filed in one of the magazines, photographs of six or seven former CJIs were on front page. Such allegations/rumours have gone up. Today, 20 years after my retirement , when I visit the residence of some of the judges of high court, I really think within myself how even after retirement, a judge of the high court can maintain such a lavish standard of living. I personally feel that the public confidence in the judiciary is getting eroded to a great extent and the common man is not prepared to respect the judges in the same manner as was the case 30–40 years back.

Justice Patnaik was also one of the judges who blocked my candidature in 1979, and he expressed his regret on the matter to me on several occasions while we were working together in Orissa High Court. He had also developed an inferiority complex, maybe because of the fact that he had realised that some undue favour had been shown to him by way of elevating him to the Supreme Court by superseding the rightful claim of so many seniors. After taking oath, whenever he visited Orissa, he used to meet me and narrate his experience in the Supreme Court, but I used to always tell him that he should not have any inferiority complex, and that this complex had developed possibly because he had never practised at the Supreme Court as an advocate, while I was regularly arguing there during my tenure in the office of advocate general, particularly during 1979–1982. He would also tell me that before his retirement, he would see to it that I should be elevated as a judge of the Supreme Court. However, the favour that had been shown to him did not last long, and he died in a car accident during the summer vacation of 1991 while driving.

R.C. Patnaik was only the third judge from Orissa High Court to be elevated as judge of Supreme Court in 1991. In 40 years of existence of the Supreme Court, only three elevations from Orissa High Court! In my view, it is because the judges of Orissa High Court were neglected, and they do not have any lobby being a smaller high court with a small judge strength. If merit is considered to be the sole criterion for elevation of a judge to the Supreme Court from a high court, then, in my opinion, cases of at least three or four competent persons from Orissa must be said to have been overlooked.

It was also during the tenure of Chief Justice Hansaria, when M.N. Venkatachaliah was the CJI, that he wanted to frame some guidelines to hold in-house enquiry against any judge of the high courts or the Supreme Court in the event of a complaint against any one of them. A committee was constituted to formulate the code of conduct for a judge, and that committee was headed by the senior-most judge of the Supreme Court, Justice Pandian. Justice J.S. Verma was also a member, and three high court judges were chosen. One was Justice Pariporanan from Kerala, the second was Chief Justice Swami, who was originally from Karnataka and was the chief justice of Tamil Nadu, and the third was myself. We had a couple meetings in Delhi and Madras, and finally formulated the so-called ethics code with the title *Restatement of the Code of Conduct of the Judges of High Court and Supreme Court.*

Sometimes in 1992, Chief Justice Hansaria once asked me whether I would like to be transferred as a judge to Delhi High Court. I answered in the negative and stated that since my posting as chief justice of a high court was already due, being the senior-most pusine judge of Orissa High Court, and since there was no judge from Orissa posted as chief justice of a high court, I would not mind if I was sent as chief justice of any high court. This statement of mine was misconstrued to mean that I refused to go out of Orissa, which I got to know only long after, in 1994, when a very senior lawyer told me that when he had met CJI Venkatachaliah, he was informed that the chief justiceship of Delhi High Court had been offered to me, and I had refused. Such misconceptions arise because the CJI does not interact with the judge concerned but sends a message through an emissary, and, in my opinion, this is not proper. I continued as senior-most puisne judge of Orissa High Court till 1995, and for a period of more than four years, there was no chief justice from Orissa High Court nor was there any person in the Supreme Court. While I was a judge of the Supreme Court, there was an unwritten convention that as far as practicable, each high court should be represented in the Supreme Court, and this was the convention when the total judge strength was only 25. But now, even with the increase of strength to 34, there is nobody from Orissa High Court as a judge in the Supreme Court for the last 3 years. This is why I have stated earlier that the small high court and the judges thereof are often overlooked. This was the case in the past and it also continues to be so in the present.

Chief Justice Hansaria was appointed as judge of the Supreme Court sometime in December 1993, and in his place Justice G.T. Nanavati from Gujarat High Court was appointed as chief justice of Orissa High Court. Temperament wise, he was not a relief-oriented judge, and as such was not liked by members of the Bar. In criminal cases, he was so pro-prosecution that acquitting an accused was not possible for him. He was a true Gujarati so far as finance was concerned, and used to scrutinize thoroughly the entitlements of a judge. I recall a funny incident in this regard. It so happened that a judge on being appointed in Madhya Pradesh High Court had been transferred to Orissa High Court. At that time, a judge was entitled to get Rs 20,000 for furnishing the bungalow. Prior to Chief Justice Nanavati, the furnishing of office room, including table, chair and almirah, was not included therein, but the Chief Justice interpreted the rule to mean that the furnishing of the office room should also be included therein. As a result, there would be no money left for the judge to get his bungalow furnished. This was also a harsh decision. The judge, therefore, requested me to have a word with the Chief Justice. As the chief justice was newly appointed and I had no acquaintance with him earlier, I did not like to tell him anything, and I thought he would take it as interference with his administrative powers. I, therefore, advised the new judge to direct the registry to take away all the books and almirahs from the office room and instead ask his secretary to indent 100 to 150 books daily from the library. He did so, and the expenses of bringing the book and taking them back became so much that in seven days' time, Chief Justice Nanavati withdrew his earlier order and held that furnishing the office room would not be included in the designated expense. The Chief Justice and his wife were very friendly and had a nice time in Orissa, which was very short period of seven–eight months. I became his colleague in the Supreme Court, and even after his retirement, I remained in touch with him till he expired two years ago.

After him, Justice V.A. Mohta from Bombay High Court was appointed as chief justice of Orissa High Court. He was a fine gentleman, always jovial in nature. He was a relief-oriented judge, unlike Justice Nanavati, so the members of the Bar were quite happy. One incident during his tenure is worth mentioning: a senior judge of Orissa High Court was unusually delaying in delivering judgement on matters which had been heard. The Supreme Court was repeatedly reminding the Chief Justice to send the data as to which judge heard how many cases and how many of them had been finally disposed of. Chief Justice Mohta was feeling embarrassed to pointedly tell the senior judge about the same, and he therefore, requested me to put in a word to the said judge since he knew that the judge was very close to me. I, however, replied that he would take it amiss if I would tell him, saying further that it would be better if the Chief Justice called him and made the request himself. I also suggested that on file, he may be given some administrative duties for 15 days, and he may be requested to utilize the time in delivering the judgement in the cases which he had heard. The chief justice followed my suggestion and requested the judge to dispose of the pending case by writing the judgement. The decision yielded good result, and he could dispose of most of the pending cases.

In 1995 January, Chief Justice Mohta called me and the next senior judge of Orissa High Court to his residence one day. The purpose was the suggestion of names for the elevation as judges of the high court. As we reached his residence, he himself suggested five names from the bar and the name of a district judge. I immediately agreed with four names for elevation from the Bar and also the district judge, but about the fifth man, I indicated that he was quite young and so should wait for some more time. Chief Justice Mohta then said unless younger people from the Bar were elevated as judges of the high court, it would not be possible for judges of Orissa High Court to be elevated to the Supreme Court. Hearing this, I immediately agreed to the fifth person also, and all the six names were finalised within a period of 10 minutes. I had heard that in different high courts finalisation of name by the collegium took much longer in the absence of consensus among members. In my view, if the collegium of a high court, consisting of the chief justice and two senior-most judges, dispassionately considers the case of elevation from the members of the Bar with the sole object of sending good and meritorious persons for elevation, keeping in mind the interest of the court, then there should be no reason as to why consensus cannot be reached among the collegium members.

During the tenure of Chief Justice Mohta, an interesting case was relating to the department of mines in the Government of Orissa. In that case, the parties were Government of Orissa in the mining department as well as the Orissa Mining Corporation. The secretary of mining was also the chairman of the Mining Corporation. On behalf of the corporation, he had engaged a very senior and well-known advocate of the Bar and also sent an instruction that this advocate would represent both the state as well as corporation in the case, and a copy of that letter was sent to the advocate general. The advocate general, who was my teacher in law college, met me and conveyed the humiliation he was feeling on receiving the letter from the secretary. When advocate general of Orissa came to my chamber, I, however, requested him to prepare for the case even so. After the case began, the petitioner lawyer argued and continued for the whole day, and the respondents were to begin the submission on the next day. Since there were a number of respondents in the case, I enquired as to who were the lawyers to argue and got the reply that according to the order of the government, the senior-most lawyer engaged by the corporation would argue for both the state and the corporation. I told the so-called senior-most lawyer that when the advocate general had entered appearance on behalf of the state, and state was the party before the court, he had right of pre audience, and therefore, the court would hear the advocate general first and, if necessary, would hear the others thereafter. Thus, the advocate general got the opportunity of arguing first before us. In course of time, the constitutional post of advocate general is losing its importance primarily because lawyers are being appointed as advocate generals by lobbying and not on account of their own competence. The post of attorney general in the Supreme Court and the posts of advocate general in each high court are the most prestigious appointments in the legal circle. If the importance is gradually declining it is because of the conduct of the appointees themselves.

Another memorable incident during this time was a civil revision hearing on a Friday, when a fairly young lawyer entered my courtroom and interrupted court while I was in the midst of some other matter. I immediately told the lawyer that this was highly improper and he should wait till the matter got over. After about 15 minutes, when the matter got over, the lawyer mentioned the matter and told me that a civil revision against the interim order of the court of subordinate judge by which the annual general meeting of the company had been stayed had been filed. He also mentioned that the chief justice had asked him to mention it to me. I told the lawyer I would take up the matter only after I finished all the matter listed for admission that day and not before. My admission list got over within half an hour, and then I took up that matter, and after hearing the lawyer for about five minutes, I passed an order permitting the general body meeting to be held as scheduled and that any decision taken thereon would not be given effect without the permission of the court.

After about 15 minutes of my passing the order, a senior lawyer engaged on behalf of the company appeared before me and stated that his office had entered a caveat on behalf of the respondent in that case, and therefore, the court could not have passed any order without hearing him. I enquired from the registry and found that, in fact, a caveat had been entered. So, I told him the case would be reheard and called for the advocate who had filed the civil revision. I told the senior lawyer that no adverse order had been passed and it was only an order permitting the holding of general body meeting, since people from different parts of the state had already arrived and there could be dislocation, but all the same, I permitted him to argue the matter. I heard him for about half an hour and then stated I did not see any reason to change my order, since the order was an innocuous one and the decision taken therein could not be given effect without the permission of the court. The senior lawyer then flared up and submitted that in his long career as advocate of more than 45 years, no court had ever stopped him for arguing, and therefore, the court may record as to when he started his argument and when he was asked by court to stop. Such a request from the senior lawyer appeared to me to be very unusual, since it is the court that decides the manner in which the proceeding is to continue and not the lawyer. In fact, I felt a bit embarrassed. I then told the lawyer that I had been a judge for 11 years and no lawyer had made a request in the manner in which the request was being made, and as such I was unable to accede to the request. I also told him that if he was agonised by the order, he could very well approach the higher forum against the same. After conclusion of the matter, I really felt very uneasy, as the senior lawyer was my senior in whose chamber I had worked for about six years when I began as a lawyer in the profession. This event disturbed me to an extent that I remained distracted throughout the day. I came back home and was resting, when the same lawyer reached my residence and told me that he was sorry for what had happened in court and he ought not to have said so. I also told him that he should forget what happened in court, since the court was a place where each party was playing its allotted role and nobody should take it seriously. Then we spent about an hour reminiscing our past days.

Yet another case which I cannot forget was the constitutional validity of the Orissa Rural Employment, Education and Production (OREEP) Act 1992, which the Orissa legislature had passed, levying tax on minerals for development of the villages. The revenue collected per year used to be Rs 400 crores. The mine owners challenged the constitutional validity of the legislation inter-alia on the ground that the Orissa legislature did not have the power to make legislation on minerals. The stance of the government, however, was that it was the legislation on land, not minerals, and was aimed at improvement of education in the rural area. The case came up before Chief Justice Mohta and brother Justice R.K. Patra, but as the chief justice was to retire shortly thereafter, he sent the matter to my bench, sitting with R.K. Patra, and, accordingly, the case was listed before us. There were large number of petitioners, since several writ petitions had been clubbed together. Mostly they were mine owners, and eminent lawyers from Delhi and Calcutta had been engaged along with several lawyers of Orissa High Court. The chief arguing counsels on behalf of petitioners were Senior Advocate K.N. Parasaran, Senior Advocate Shanti

Bhushan, who was law minister in PM Morarji Desai's cabinet, Amal Ganguly from Delhi and Smaraditya Pal from Calcutta, to name a few. On behalf of the state, the advocate general was appearing. Usually, I did not read brief of cases fixed for hearing at home, as I did not want to go to court with a pre-conceived notion. I always preferred to hear the counsel for the parties and then take the decision of my own. But as the case involved was a heavy matter with so many outside counsels coming, I had glanced through one of the writ petitions. When the case began on a Monday, I wanted to know as to how much time the case would consume and, for that purpose, asked the counsel as to the number of days they would require to argue. Since Mr Shanti Bhushan was for the petitioner in the first case, he stated that he would require at least nine hearing days for his submissions. Mr Parasaran wanted four days. Several lawyers present there wanted at least two–three days each, and all in all, it came to 21 days for completion of the petitioners' case. The advocate general wanted seven days for his argument. The petitioners' counsel wanted at least four–five days for reply, and, in all, the number of days came to about 32–33 days. There was also a prayer that the case not be heard on Fridays. With the aforesaid time schedule in mind, the case began, and Mr Bhushan started his argument. By about 3:30 pm on the first day, I summarised the possible viewpoints of the arguments that could be argued on behalf of petitioner and enquired as to any other angle on which the counsel would argue. Mr Shanti Bhushan frankly said that he would not argue from any other angle. Therefore, I requested that Mr Shanti Bhushan should conclude his submission the next day and also told the other senior counsels that they need not repeat what Mr Shanti Bhushan had argued and could urge any special angle in which they wanted to argue. Mr Bhushan concluded submission on the second day. Mr Parasaran argued for one day, and all other counsels for the petitioner concluded their submission within two more days. Thus, the entire argument on behalf of the petitioners stood concluded within four days. The case was not taken up on Friday, as prayed for in the beginning. During the next week, the advocate general for the state began his reply and concluded within three days. On the fourth day, the response from the counsel for the petitioner was given and the hearing stood concluded on the eighth day. We had also permitted the counsels for the parties to submit written synopsis of argument within one week from the date of conclusion of the case.

The judgement was delivered three weeks thereafter. We had taken the decision that though the name of the legislation purports to be one for the benefit of rural education and appears to be levy of tax on the land, but, in fact, it is a levy of tax on mineral, and consequently, the Orissa legislature does not have power to make the law in question and such a legislation can only be made by Parliament. We struck down the Act by holding the same to be invalid and directed the state government to refund the tax that had been collected. One day after the judgement was delivered, the advocate general came to my residence and said that the CM was very sad that the act was struck down, since the Orissa government would lose around Rs 400 crores per year and there was the liability to refund the tax. I told the advocate general if the government felt that our decision was erroneous, they should approach the Supreme Court against our judgement. In fact, the state moved the Supreme Court, but ultimately the apex court dismissed the appeal.

In the early part of January 1995, on my request, my classmate in school as well as in college, Sourindra Bose, who was the principal chief conservator of forests, had organised a trip to Gahirmatha to see the nesting of Olive Ridley turtles. He rang me up from Bhubaneswar and said he would pick me up. When I entered his car, I found that another classmate of mine, Priyambada, who was a zoology professor in Ravenshaw College, sitting in the front seat. She was also a very good dancer and was mainly responsible for bringing Odissi dance to the national stage. Seeing her, I made some joke, and all three of us made our way towards the destination in the white ambassador car of the chief conservator of forests. We drove for about 70–80 km to a place beyond Patamundai, where we boarded the motorised steamer and reached Gahirmatha. Reaching there, we found couple of other visitors on the seashore, accommodated in camps. The arrangement was really fine, and as soon as evening descended, we found Olive Ridley turtles emerging from the sea on the beach to lay eggs. It was a wonderful scene that can never be forgotten. One must see this to realise how beautiful it is. One turtle can lay about 100–150 eggs. That evening census recorded around 1,65,000 turtles on the beach. We spent a nice evening and remained on the beach till 10 pm and then retired for the night after dinner. The next morning, we left after breakfast. On our return, Priyambada casually remarked that since we had returned after seeing the Kurmaavatar (an avatar of Lord Vishnu) I was bound to be promoted soon. Her words came true within four months when I was appointed as chief justice of Patna High Court.

Chief justice Mohta retired in the last week of April 1995. The state of Orissa was inclined to appoint him as chairman of the Human Rights Commission, but he did not agree and instead set up a private practice in the Supreme Court and was a successful practitioner till his death. As the senior-most puisne judge of Orissa High Court, I was appointed as the acting chief justice. While I was the acting chief justice, sometime in the first week of May 1995, Justice Hansaria rang me up from Delhi and told me not to take up any big matter, as I would likely be appointed as the chief justice of Patna High Court. At that point of time, there existed vacancies of chief justices in three high courts, namely Patna, Bangalore and Hyderabad. Somehow, I had a poor impression about Patna city, especially the law-and-order situation in Bihar, and instead preferred a posting in Bangalore. With that desire in mind when I enquired from the Justice Hansaria as to whether decision had already been taken regarding who would go as chief justice of Karnataka High Court, the answer I got was that since I had already refused the post of a chief justice once, if I refused it this time my name would not be considered in the future. I replied that I was not refusing, only enquiring.

On 18 May 1995, my appointment as chief justice of Patna High Court was notified. Orissa High Court was closing for summer vacation on 19 May. Accordingly, I decided that I would take oath in Patna only after Patna High Court reopened after the summer vacation and conveyed the same to the registrar of Patna High Court. To my great surprise, I received a large number of telephone calls from the senior judges of Patna High Court requesting me to join immediately. On my query as to what was the urgency for which such request was being made, the answer was that the brother judges feared that the acting chief justice, even within a short span, would take several decisions not in the interest of the high court. I could not find any justification for this explanation, since any decision taken by the acting chief justice could be changed when the permanent chief justice assumed office. After two–three days, I received a telephone call from Justice N.P. Singh, a judge of the Supreme Court originally belonging to Patna High Court. When I told him that I would like to join after the summer vacation, he made a frantic request that I should take oath before Patna High Court closed for summer vacation. I was thus compelled to leave Orissa on 23 May, and 25 May was fixed as my date of oath-taking.

Twelve years of life as a judge in Orissa High Court was quite happy and smooth. The government accommodation was very spacious, with a beautiful lawn and garden in the front and a kitchen garden at the back. The court work was not heavy and became much simpler after two years as judge. The evenings used to be really enjoyable with friends, more particularly my doctor friends. Saturdays and Sundays were spent with relatives in town. Short vacations were utilised for visiting nearby scenic places with children. During this period, all my children completed their schooling and higher studies. My eldest son started his job with Tata and also got married on 20 January 1995. My second son was still pursuing his MBA at the Xavier Institute of Management. I and my wife could fulfil a life's desire of going abroad. Of course, the tragedy was that I lost my father in 1985.

# Chief Justice at Patna High Court

I left for Patna with my wife and my younger brother by Puri–Howrah Express on the evening of 23 May 1995. That day, the railway station at Cuttack was packed with eminent lawyers and judges of the high court. A couple of ministers were also there to bid farewell to me. I, infact, became slightly emotional at the thought of leaving the city where I had spent all my life so far, and resolved to come back to this city after my retirement. I was, however, praying that the number of years I would continue as judge should pass smoothly. When the train reached Howrah Station, we were taken to the Great Eastern Hotel, which was then the State Guest House of the Bengal government, and after lunch, we took a little rest and boarded the Calcutta–Delhi Rajdhani, which would stop at Patna. The deputy registrar protocol of Patna High Court had come to Orissa and was travelling with us in the train. One joint registrar of Orissa High Court was also travelling with us. We reached Patna around 8 pm, and I found that at least 300–400 people had assembled to welcome me. I was indeed surprised, since in Orissa I had never seen such a huge gathering when a chief justice or a judge arrived from outside the state. Most of the judges, senior lawyers and many citizens were there in the gathering, and each one of them was putting a garland on me. The crowd gathered said out aloud, 'We need such judgement.' I could not follow what they wanted, and upon my query, a judge told me that they were referring to a recent judgement I had given in Orissa against the police and government. I remembered then that the then Orissa CM had made a statement that the person accused of offence under 498A IPC, involving torture of wife for want of dowry, should be arrested and brought with an iron chain on the neck and the leg. The then DG of Police issued a circular on that basis and a petition had been filed challenging the circular. After hearing not only had I set aside the circular but I had also indicted the DG of Police and observed that he should not be allowed to continue in his position. That judgement had been delivered only two days before I had left Orissa. But people at Patna got to know of it even before I reached Patna.

From the railway station, we were taken to the chief justice's bungalow, where we spent the night. In the morning, I got up and went around the bungalow, which was spread over more than 9 acres of land, and there were at least eight–nine big rooms, including six–seven bedrooms. There was a huge living room and a fairly big dining hall. The dining hall itself had a dining table meant for 20–22 persons, and there was a huge veranda outside, which was so big that a party for 100 people could easily be arranged there. The property also had a sprawling lawn with rose bushes. Also, there was a small tank and on the front side, there was a huge vacant space. The bungalow was originally the palace of the maharaja of Darbhanga, and when Bihar and Orissa were declared as a separate province from Bengal, the British administration purchased that building from the maharaja to turn into the residence of the governor of the newly formed province. It was only after the construction of governor's official residence, the building was given to the high court for being used as residence of the chief justice. The total area covered more than 14 acres initially, 5 acres from which was given away for the construction of an All-India Radio campus by Justice K.B.N. Singh.

On 25 May, the swearing-in ceremony was held in Raj Bhavan, whereas in Orissa, the swearing-in of a chief justice was usually held in the high court campus. Inside Raj Bhavan, all the judges of the court with their spouses, the CM and members of state cabinet and many senior advocates were present. Lalu Prasad Yadav was the then CM of Bihar. Post the oath ceremony and the small tea party that was organised on the occasion, I went straight to the high court and held court. At this, I heard later, that the CM had casually remarked that at this rate, I would shortly leave for the Supreme Court in Delhi, and so it happened, but I will come to that later.

Reaching the high court building, I was introduced to all the judges, and as far as I remember, there were about 30 judges in Patna High Court at that time. There was a circuit bench of Patna High Court at Ranchi, which was then part of the Bihar, and there were about 10–12 judges at Ranchi. Finding the judge strength to be so high, for a moment, I was quite nervous, since in my parent court in Orissa there were only 10–11 judges by the time I had left. I then asked the registry to make my cause list for the day along with the senior-most judge available there; it was Mr. B.L. Yadav, who had been transferred from Allahabad to Patna and was the acting chief justice before I took oath. Since I had taken charge as a new chief justice, my courtroom, though quite huge, was packed with lawyers, who had possibly gathered to gauge the attitude and temperament of the new chief justice.

When I sat in the court that day, I was reminded of a casual remark made by the then chief justice of Orissa High Court in 1964 when he was transferred from Orissa to Patna. In a dinner organised by members of the Bar in honour of the transferred chief justice, he had observed that the Orissa High Court Bar was nothing but a dignified district court Bar. He was overjoyed when he received his transfer order to Patna as chief justice, the reason being after Orissa, a small high court with just four judges, he would be going to head Patna High Court, which had at least 40 judges. I was then a young lawyer, and felt offended by such a remark, more so because it was improper to make such comment at a dinner for his felicitation. But no senior lawyer made any objection to such remark. On my last working day in Orissa High Court, I had stated in court that had the learned chief justice who made such comment been alive I would have rung him up and informed him that a member of the so-called dignified district Bar has been appointed as chief justice of Patna High Court.

Amongst the pre-Independence high courts in the country, Patna High Court had a very good reputation. Justice B.P. Sinha from Patna High Court was the 6th CJI in the Supreme Court, and when the total strength of judges in the Supreme Court was eight, including the CJI, three judges from Patna High Court were in the Supreme Court. But after passage of time and growth of several high courts in the country after India got independence, the aura and importance of Patna High Court declined, and the judges of Patna High Court suffered the same ignominy and neglect in terms of elevation to the Supreme Court as the judges of the smaller high courts in the country.

The very first or second matter was a case where the appellant had not paid the court fee within the time fixed. The lawyer representing the appellant stated this fact and prayed for an extension of time to pay the court fee. When I asked the counsel as to where the application was, he stated that there was no application on file but it was an oral application. I asked the counsel to look at section 149 of Code of Civil Procedure. At that stage, a senior lawyer present within my court submitted that though the statute required an application to be filed, the convention had been that on an oral application by the counsel, the court granted time. I told the senior counsel that I was not bound by so-called convention, if at all there was any, and that I could only go by the provisions of the Code or a decision of the court or of the Supreme Court on the point. Since there weren't any such decision either of Patna High Court or of the Supreme Court, and Section 149 of CPC required an application to be filed by the party seeking extension of time, that had to be followed. There was no further deliberation thereafter, and I granted time for three days to make an application under Section 149 of CPC. The reason behind mentioning this fact is to indicate that the local Bar might have thought since I am from a smaller court, I would accept whatever is stated by the senior counsel as gospel truth, but I did not allow that situation to prevail.

The very first day at Pana High Court went smoothly. My friends, who had come from Orissa, though they were not conversant with law or court atmosphere, were also present in the courtroom for more than an hour to watch the proceedings. A tea party was organised for all the Bar association members at around 3 pm in the high court lawn, so I got up early to attend the same. More than 3000 lawyers attended that party.

I gathered there were three associations, namely Advocate Association, Bar Association and Lawyers' Association. The Lawyers' Association was, infact, an association of a splinter group of lawyers who withdrew from the Advocate Association and made an association for themselves. The Bar Association was the association of barristers from England, but by the time I arrived as chief justice, I don't think there were any barristers. I also went around the association hall and found it to be very congested. At the tea party, I also met my former Chief Justice H.L. Aggarwal, who introduced me to several retired judges present at the party.

When I came back home, I found at least more than 200 files kept on my office table and the Registrar General along with two other officers waiting for me. I asked the Registrar General as to why so many files required my signature. He replied that these were files relating to financial sanction of the Chief Justice in connection with official expenses of the judges of the court. When I opened the first file, I found about two pages of noting relating to expenditure of Rs 25 in connection with some official use of a judge. When I asked if the Chief Justice was required to apply his mind for sanctioning the expense of Rs 25 then what was the role of the registrar, he immediately brought out a file wherein Chief Justice Basak, from Calcutta, had passed an order requiring all financial transactions to be sanctioned by the chief justice himself. I was surprised that two other chief justices before me had also continued the same practice. I thought it was ridiculous for a chief justice of a high court to sanction such a small amount. I, therefore, in the very same file, wrote an order naming the registrar general as the sanctioning authority for all the financial transactions up to a limit of Rs 25,000. I communicated to the registrar general that if the number of files did not reduce once this order was in effect, then I would enhance the sanctioning power to Rs 50,000 or even Rs 1 lakh. The registrar then told me with some hesitation that the judges would feel aggrieved if some expenses were not sanctioned due to the strict rules. I then told him that he should not be meticulous about following the rules in letter and spirit, and in case he felt that in a given case, the expenses were highly exorbitant and rules did not permit them, then he may bring that file to me. I also told him that petty expenses need not be scrutinised thoroughly, and I would support him so long as he followed this principle. This order of mine reduced the files from 200 per day to about 10–12 per day and was a great relief to me as long as I continued in Patna.

The next day, I was informed that the judges of the high court had their own groups, mostly based on caste, as casteism was predominant in Bihar. There used to be a typed list of all the judges in the high court on my office table, and I started noting down their caste against their names. For example, against a Bhumihar judge, I noted BH, against a Kurmi judge, I noted KR, against a Brahmin judge, I noted BR, and against a Kayastha judge, I noted KA, and so on and so forth. I made the noting for my own consumption. That night, I had arranged dinner for all guests and friends who had come from Orissa as well as my family members so that I could spend time with them. My friends left for Cuttack the next day morning, and my wife and children left by train the evening of the same day.

The next day, I left my residence a bit early in order to find out whether the staff in the registry office were punctual to court. Reaching the court, I just barged into the office and found that most people had not arrived. I gathered from the registrar that the staff had an association, so I sent for the executive members of association during lunch. When they met me in my chamber, I wanted to know their grievances, and they raised quite a number of demands. At the end of the conversation, I told them that, as against so many demands, I had only one demand, namely the staff must reach office on the dot and should also leave the office on time. And a register would be maintained for attendance, where they would be required to sign, and if they were late on any day, then a red mark would indicate so, and after three red marks, they could be suspended and disciplinary proceedings initiated against them. If they agreed with this proposal and gave it in writing to me on the next day, I would certainly consider all their demands, and if found reasonable, I would try my level best to fulfil them as far as practicable. But till I left Patna in September, I did not receive any such written confirmation from them, and as such, the necessity of considering their grievances did not arise.

For a Chief Justice of any high court to be effective and successful as well as popular, it is necessary to have good relationship with a few institutions, namely, (a) the brother and sister judges (b) different associations of the advocates (c) the registry and the staff and (d) the state government. I had decided it would be my endeavour to maintain good relations with all these institutions and, with that end in view, I decided that I would visit at least two–three judges' residence every evening just to get to know them better, ascertain their temperament and also to get the feedback from them. On the third day, in the evening, the president of the subordinate judicial officers' association, who was a retired judge of the high court, met me and told me that the promotion file from the junior division to senior division was pending with the government for more than one-and-a-half years, as a result of which posts in the senior division were lying vacant. The reason for the same was that the government insisted that the reservation policy should apply, whereas the high court was of view that the rules did not provide for the reservation, and so the matter was in a deadlock. I told the gentleman that on my return from home after the summer vacation, I would meet the CM and persuade him to agree with the proposal. But he stated the CM would never agree unless reservation was made applicable. I then politely said that there was no harm in trying.

In another instance, when I entered into the chamber of brother judge, I found that it was not air-conditioned. Even though it was just May, I realised it was rather impossible to work without air-conditioning in the chamber in a hot place like Patna. I could not believe that judges of Patna High Court were working without air-conditioning in their chambers. When I asked a few other senior judges, they informed me that the government would not sanction so many ACs, and even my predecessors had tried and failed. That evening, I requested the law secretary to meet me over a cup of tea, and while taking tea, I told him that the high court needed about 40 air-conditioners to be installed in the chambers of the judges of the court, and I would expect the government's sanction within a week. I impressed upon the law secretary that he was the liaison officer between the high court and state government, and also reminded him that being the senior-most district judge in the cadre at that point of time, he should be considered for elevation to the high court, and his prompt efforts in getting the sanction of the government for the 40 air-conditioners would accelerate the question of his elevation to court. These few words really worked well and the law secretary, who was one Mr Sarkar, could manage to get the government sanction within a very short time. Mr Sarkar was elevated to the high court shortly after I left Patna.

Patna High Court closed for summer vacation on 28 May and I had planned to go back to Cuttack that very evening. I had booked my ticket from Patna to Calcutta by Danapur Express, and from Howrah to Cuttack by a train which used to leave Howrah by 3 pm and reach Cuttack around 9 pm. Before leaving my residence at Patna on 28th evening, the registrar general asked me what he would do with mangoes from a tree within the chief justice's bungalow that would ripen during the vacation. There was one tree of *langra* variety from where at least a truckload of mangoes was expected. I told him that he could collect the ripe mangoes every day and distribute the same amongst the judges of the high court and thereafter among the retired judges available in Patna. He followed my instructions religiously, and every day while in Cuttack, I used to get telephone calls from four or five judges daily thanking me for sending mangoes from my bungalow. When I reached the platform at Patna Railway Station, I found that the train was already in, but I did not find a single passenger. I could not understand the reason, and on being asked was told that only after I boarded the train would the other passengers be permitted to enter the platform. I was indeed surprised at this reply and felt that in Bihar they overdid these things, as a result of which the general public suffered unnecessarily.

During the vacation, my plan was to leave my daughter in the hostel in Cuttack, as she was in final year of BSc Honours, and return to Patna with my wife after the summer vacation. Though my daughter initially agreed, later she did not want to stay in the hostel alone. I, therefore, decided that my wife would stay with my daughter on the first floor of my Kafla house. So, I engaged a contractor to get the first floor ready, and to fix up one air-conditioner. But the contractor said the construction would not be completed within the summer vacation. I, therefore, requested my former colleague who was the acting chief justice then for permitting me to stay at the Cantonment Road bungalow for one more month, and he kindly agreed. I decided that I would come back again by the end of July or first week of August and make the necessary arrangements for shifting from the Cantonment Road bungalow to the Kafla house.

The one-month summer vacation got over very quickly, and I came back to Patna, leaving my wife and daughter at the 6, Cantonment Road bungalow. Back at Patna, I was thinking of ways to convince the CM to release the promotion file of the judicial officers. To my good luck, within a day, the CM himself wanted to meet me, and I immediately agreed and asked my private secretary to extend an invitation to the CM to meet me in the evening. The CM arrived at my residence around 6 pm and immediately revealed the purpose of his visit—he wanted to host a dinner for me. When I asked whether he had invited any of my predecessors, he replied in the negative and reasoned that since my predecessors were from South India and were not able to talk in Hindi, he had not invited them. I then enquired as to who would be the invitees to the party, to which he replied that he would invite all the judges of the high court, his law minister and the speaker of the legislative assembly. I, therefore, agreed, and he fixed up the date then and there. After that, we started discussing problems of Bihar and I offered him tea. While he was having tea, I told him I also had a request for him, to which he promptly said that a request from the chief justice was a command for him. I then told him that the high court had a file pending in the CM's office for quite some time. He immediately understood what file I was referring to and told me that this related to the promotion of the judicial officers, and he would not agree with the suggestion of high court until and unless the reservation principle was made applicable for such promotions. I then promptly replied that since the CM didn't agree to my request, I withdraw my words and would not be available for the dinner. He told me that since I had accepted the offer of his invitation, my refusal would not be correct. I replied that since the CM didn't agree to my request, I had no other alternative. He then thought for some time as to what he would do. After about 5 minutes, I reminded him that the promotion of the judicial officer was governed by a set of rules, and those rules do not prescribe any reservation. Until and unless those rules were changed, the policy of reservation could not be made available. I further told him that if the CM agreed with the suggestions and sent back the file, then I would try my best to amend the rules and provide reservation therein so that when the next round of promotions would be up for consideration, the policy of reservation would apply. He immediately understood the matter and agreed to send back the file. As he was about to leave my residence, he assured me that he would get the file released that very night. I did not take any chance and told him that our registrar general would accompany him and bring back the file personally. It was already 7 pm by then. But the CM stuck to his word. The very next day, I requested the standing committee of the high court to decide the posting of these officers, and within a day, the order of promotion together with the posting was notified in the gazette. Such quick action was taken as I was apprehensive that the CM might change his mind. At this, the judicial officers and their association were immensely pleased. About 70 officers were promoted to senior division judicial services, and the litigant public benefited from this act as vacancies were filled up. This is one instance which shows how a chief justice of a high court is required to adopt different modalities for the smooth functioning of the entire judiciary in the state.

After the 40 air-conditioners that were requested reached the high court premises, I thought that the judges would be benefitted if the air-conditioners were fixed in the office rooms at the residences instead of in the courtrooms. Other brother judges were also of the same opinion. But the registrar general and my private secretary dissuaded me from taking that decision on the ground that once the air-conditioners were fixed in the residence of the judges then there was no guarantee that it would be returned to the high court on their retirement, and it may so happen that the financial burden for that would have to be borne by the chief justice who had passed that order. I found their advice to be sound and, accordingly, ordered that the air-conditioners be fixed in the respective chambers of the judges in the high court building.

Another memorable incident that comes to mind is about a day when I was getting ready to leave my residence for court and received a telephone call from the president and secretary of one of the associations of lawyers I had mentioned earlier. They just intimated me that the members of their association were boycotting court from that day onwards. I could not understand anything, so I requested that they meet me in my chamber in the high court. I was so perplexed that instead of taking my breakfast, I left for the court immediately. Upon query I found that prior to summer vacation, a bail application that was being argued by one of the members of the association was dismissed by a judge of the high court whereafter the lawyer made a comment on the ability of the judge, stating that he was not fit to become a magistrate.

The court, on that account, had initiated the contempt proceeding and the matter was listed for hearing on the day. I replied that the judge who had initiated the proceeding by issuing notice had committed a mistake. If I would have been in his position then I would have taken cognizance, and on hearing the contemnor, would have awarded punishment and asked the police to take the contemner to the prison from the court itself. The president and secretary stated that lawyer undoubtedly had committed contempt but what they wanted to impress upon the judge was that the contemner would beg apology in court and that the apology be accepted and proceeding dropped. I replied that the apology should be to the court where the matter was pending and not before me. But the president informed me that the judge would not accept it, and it was for that reason that they requested me to persuade the particular judge. I replied that if I intervened in any manner, then I would be committing contempt but would still put in a word, though without any assurances. With these words, I asked the lawyers to go to the court. However, before I did anything, since I was new to the institution, I wanted to consult a few senior judges of the court regarding the matter. To my surprise, none of the judges expressed any opinion and told me, on the other hand, that I could take whatever step I saw fit. I had no acquaintance with the judge in question, and I did not know what type of man he was, still, I sent for him to my chamber. In fact, at that point of time, my brain stopped working, since strike by the lawyers would be a slur on my reputation. The judge in question had not reached the court by then, so I waited for him, sending word that my court would start 15 minutes late. The learned judge reached my chamber in the next few minutes and I discussed the matter with him. I also told him that the lawyer had undoubtedly committed contempt and the contempt proceeding was the right decision on his part. I also assured the judge that whatever decision he took, he would have my full support. At the same time, I told him that if I would have been in his position then I would have accepted the apology of the contemner and dropped the proceeding so as to avoid any unpleasant situation. He finally told me that he would think over the matter. I also advised him that he could adjourn the matter on that day so that he had some time to reflect on it and take a decision on the next day. As a result, the matter was adjourned. On the next day, the alleged contemner, tendered unqualified apology in writing and promised to never repeat such a behaviour. The judge then accepted the apology and dropped the proceeding. This came as a great relief to me and I thanked the Almighty for having saved me from a great embarrassment. Strike by the lawyer association, even on the most unreasonable grounds, speaks a lot about the efficiency of the chief justice and his administration.

In the month of July, I had planned to move to the circuit bench at Ranchi for a week and thereafter travel to Cuttack, taking leave for a couple days so that I could help my wife and daughter move to our Kafla house. While I was holding court at Ranchi, I found two lawyers whose efficiency in arguing their respective cases caught my attention. I called them to my chamber and told them that on my return to Patna I would process for their elevation, but I would have to take the views of the members of collegium on the matter. I did casually consult the members of collegium about the two lawyers, and they were agreeable. But before any formal meeting and formal decision could be taken, I was shifted out of Patna on being elevated as a judge of the Supreme Court. Nevertheless, I had kept a note regarding the competence of those two lawyers and, in fact, they were elevated as judges of the high court during the tenure of my successor, and one of them also became a judge of the Supreme Court and has retired in the meantime. He is, however, no more in this world.

I am mentioning this fact to indicate that competence and ability of the person can be judged even from a single appearance, if the consideration is made dispassionately.

When I was holding court at Ranchi, the district judge had requested me to make a short visit to the district court, but I had politely replied that would only be possible on my next visit to Ranchi and not during that week. However, on Friday, I got up from the court at noon, and without telling anybody, asked my brother judge who was sitting with me to accompany me to the district court building for an unscheduled inspection. There, I found that even though it was noon, the district judge was not present in court. I went round and found many other judicial officers to be absent. Within 15 minutes, the district judge appeared. But before his arrival, the members of the Bar had apprised me as to how irregular the district judge was. I told the district judge that when the chief justice was holding court in Ranchi if he could come to court late by one-and-a-half hours, then I could well imagine what he would be doing when the chief justice was away in Patna. At this, the district judge started crying. I told him that he would be placed under suspension and disciplinary proceedings would be taken up against him, knowing fully well that could only be done by full court and not by the chief justice alone. This was just to give a piece of my mind to the judge. Ultimately, I gave him a warning and told him if I ever heard that he continued to be irregular in coming to court and did not follow punctuality in sitting on court then he would definitely have to face disciplinary proceedings. That warning did work, and so long as I was chief justice at Patna, I used to get feedback that the district judge was very punctual. I do not know what happened after I left Patna.

I left Ranchi by car and stayed at Jamshedpur for the night in the circuit house. The district collector and the superintendent of police met me in the circuit house and enquired about the time of my departure the next morning. I told them I would be leaving at 8 am. As scheduled, I left at 8 am, and before reaching the check gate at Jamsola, I found all vehicles standing in a row for more than 2–3 km. I thought probably there had been some accident, but reaching Jamsola check gate I learnt that under the order of superintendent of police, movement of vehicle had been stopped from 7 am from both sides, resulting in a plethora of stranded vehicles on both sides. I really felt sorry, since so many people suffered on account of my visit. Police in Bihar really behave in a high-handed manner, and the administration also approves of the same. At the check gate, the Bihar pilot and escort party were supposed to go back and I was to proceed with the Orissa pilot; in Orissa there used to be no escort to follow the car of the chief justice. Seeing only one pilot van, the protocol officer, who was in the car following my car, insisted that Bihar Police accompany me till Cuttack, but I emphatically told them that I would manage to travel even without any pilot vehicle and at no cost I would permit Bihar Police to escort me. With these strong words, the Bihar Police and protocol staff went back, and I proceeded on my way to Cuttack. That day, the sight of trees and people of my own state gave me such immense pleasure. And when I reached Cuttack around 2 pm, the lunch I had in my 6, Cantonment Road house was pure bliss.

The next day, when I went to our Kafla house, I found the first floor had been made ready for occupation. On Tuesday, we left the 6, Cantonment Road bungalow and moved to the first floor of our Kafla house, and on Wednesday, I left for Patna by train. The car was brought back to Patna by one orderly peon, and also brought my dog. At Kafla, we had only one help, and my wife was not only cooking but also was doing all other miscellaneous chores. Those days, since I had not arranged any car for them, she used to move by rickshaw. But she never complained, and I admire her for her silent support and resilience. Sometimes, being engrossed with the workload, we forget these small things. In retrospect,

I can say that it was a mistake on my part for having decided to let my wife and daughter stay in our Kafla house, unaware of the difficulty they would face.

After returning to Patna, I continued with my evening visits to the judges' residence, but even till the time I left Patna I could not visit all of them. My aforesaid decision was not only to have a cordial relationship with all the brother judges of the court but also to know their likes and dislikes, any factionalism existing amongst the judges, and their temperament and attitude towards the members of the Bar as well as the litigant public. So far as listing in the court was concerned, I had asked the registry to make my list with another judge in order of seniority and change it after every two days, the purpose being, I would be able to assess their individual ability to deal with the type of cases. I also asked the registry to list all branches of cases—constitutional, civil and criminal—in my court. This was an interim arrangement I made; so that I could constitute appropriate benches for different type of cases to be handled by the judges. I was of the view—and I am still of that view—that if the right type of cases are not listed before the bench, then unnecessarily a longer time will be taken for disposal of the matter. For example, criminal cases should be listed before judges who had practice on the criminal side when they were lawyers, and similarly, civil cases should be listed before those who had civil practice, and constitutional matter before those who had experience with constitutional matters.

In the month of July, I also visited Delhi to take part in the meeting of the selection committee for selecting a vice chancellor of Sambalpur University in Orissa as its chairman. I was appointed while I was a judge in Orissa, and even after my transfer to Patna, the chancellor requested me to continue in the post. I also thought of meeting the Union law minister and request him for enhancing the judge strength of Patna High Court so that pendency of cases in the court could be tackled smoothly. When I met the law minister, he readily agreed to enhance the judge strength of Patna High Court. The meeting was very cordial, and before I left his residence, he told me that I should meet CJI before I leave for Patna. When I told him that CJI was away in some foreign country, he replied that he would come back the next day, so I should postpone my visit for a day and meet the CJI. I thought to myself that if the CJI asked me why I missed court for one day what answer would I give. However, since the law minister had requested me, I changed my ticket from a morning flight to one in the evening so that I would not miss one more day. The next day, I requested the private secretary of the CJI for a meeting, but he replied that since CJI had returned late at night, he was sleeping, and that I would be informed of the time of meeting as soon as he was available. However, that call never came, and I left Bihar Bhavan around 2 pm to catch my evening flight. After reaching Patna, I contacted the law minister on telephone and apprised him of the circumstances under which I could not meet the CJI. He expressed his displeasure and told me that while chief justices of different high courts were eager to meet the CJI, I should have waited for one more day. I politely told him that, as I had missed the court work for one day on the account, I did not want to miss one more day, particularly when I had no work with the CJI.

I am told that the CJI these days prefer that the chief justices of high courts meet him often. I can't imagine for what purpose. I learnt that when one of the CJIs visited a particular state, the chief justice of the high court concerned had taken leave on account of his daughter's marriage and was absent but, on the insistence of CJI, was compelled to return to his headquarters. Years back, sometime in 1981, when the CJI visited Orissa High Court, the then chief justice of Orissa High Court accompanied him from Bhubaneswar to Cuttack in the CJI's saloon, and this was not appreciated and lot of comments came out in the newspaper criticising the conduct of the chief justice of Orissa High Court. Usually, when the CJI makes a visit to any state, the registrar of the high court and the home secretary of the government receive him at the airport. How quickly the time changes! In my opinion, the CJI should never expect the chief justice of the high court to receive him at the airport, as that would be denigrating the status of the chief justice of the high court.

An interesting full court meeting at Patna is worth mention here. Few days before that meeting, the standing committee of which I was also the chairman had taken a decision to give compulsory retirement to one of the district judges who belonged to a particular caste, essentially on the ground that his reputation was not good and his integrity was doubtful. In the meeting of the standing committee when I saw that his character roll had been endorsed to be excellent, I asked the judges on what basis they had suggested compulsory retirement, and the reply was that all of them were aware of the issue of integrity with respect to the said district judge. I was not agreeable to sign the decision, but I was told that he was such a person that he should not be allowed to continue. Reluctantly, I signed the decision as a chairman of the standing committee, but I told them that in the event of the question being raised about the correctness of this decision in full court meeting, I would certainly tell the brother judges about the circumstance under which I, as chairman, have had to sign that decision. In the event, two senior-most judges of the court narrated before me as to how my predecessor was unhappy with the proceeding of the full court, since the judges came to blows on the basis of casteism. In the agenda list for the full court meeting, the first agenda was the confirmation of the decision of the standing committee relating to compulsory retirement of the district judge. There were about 15 items in the agenda. Hearing about my predecessor's predicament, I became really nervous and thought to myself as to how to face the situation. In the full court meeting, all the judges from Ranchi were expected to be in attendance. When the meeting started at 10:30 am, since that was my first full court meeting in Patna High Court, I gave an introductory speech in the beginning. I welcomed all the brother judges. I also apprised them of what I had heard from colleagues as to the predicament of my predecessor and further stated that I would permit all discussion so long as the discussions were relevant to the topic of the agenda and the level of discussion be as it ought to be amongst the judges of a high court and I would not tolerate any pandemonium in such discussion. I closed my speech with a note of caution reminding them that I would continue as chief justice of the court for more than five years. The last sentence worked very well, and all the items in the agenda could be concluded within half an hour, without any discussion from any quarter. And since lunch was to be served at 1 pm, we had to wait for more than an hour, which we spent chatting. On that day, I offered my gratitude to Lord Jagannath for having come to my rescue.

I liked the vibe in Patna High Court very much. There, I introduced some of my ideas, which yielded good results. Earlier a judge who heard bail applications could dispose of only 15–16 matters in a day. I told the brother judges that the order on the bail application need not be elaborate and they should hear for 10–15 minutes and dispose of the matter with short (small) orders. Following this method, a judge could dispose of 50 applications per day. I also introduced a system by which at the end of the week, a list would be prepared and would be circulated amongst all the judges indicating which judge had disposed of how many cases. This was a practice that had been introduced by Chief Justice G.K. Mishra in

Orissa High Court. After introducing that system in Patna, I noticed that the number of disposals went up. I had requested the government for the construction of a new Bar Association building to accommodate the members of the Bar. The proposal was pending for more than a month, but when it was made known that I would be leaving for Supreme Court soon, not only was the proposal sanctioned by the CM but the location of that proposed building also could be fixed within the high court campus, and the foundation stone was laid by me in the presence of the CM, and all this had been arranged on the initiative of the CM himself. The CM, as I have mentioned, was Mr Lalu Prasad Yadav. I found him to be a shrewd man. If he wanted to get something done, he could do it in one day, and if he didn't want to do it, the file remained pending for years together.

Towards the third week of August, I received a call from Justice Hansaria, who was in the Supreme Court then, intimating me of my elevation to the Supreme Court and that I should not take up any big matter for hearing. Three days thereafter, a brother judge from Patna met me and told me that there were two vacancies in the Supreme Court and the chief justice of Gujarat and chief justice of Karnataka High Courts were being elevated, and I was not considered. I, infact, did not attach much importance to it, since I had decided to take things in my stride. But two days thereafter, the CJI himself congratulated me and informed me about my elevation. That evening, I asked my wife to come over to Patna as I wanted her to accompany me to Delhi.

That evening, I grew nostalgic thinking of all the events in my life that culminated to this day. How my childhood desire of becoming a doctor and serve my villagers could not be fulfilled because I neglected my studies at the intermediate level. How I gave up a well-paying job in a multinational and decided to embrace the hardship of becoming a lawyer. How the reputation I earned as lawyer made the then chief justice of Orissa High Court recommend my name for elevation to the high court when I was only 41 years old. But when that recommendation was not accepted, I had thought to myself that even if I became a judge at later point of time, I may not get the opportunity of being elevated to the Supreme Court. And four years thereafter, when I was elevated as a judge, I took it for granted that I would retire as a chief justice of high court somewhere in the country. Even in becoming a chief justice, there was delay on the part of the appointing authority, and for four years, I continued as the senior-most puisne judge of Orissa High Court. In May 1995, when I was appointed as the chief justice of Patna High Court, I had never imagined that I would ever be appointed to the Supreme Court that year itself, and so when I received the congratulatory message from the CJI, I became certain of one thing, namely, destiny plays a role in every man's life and, as far as I was concerned, I was destined to end my career in the apex court of India.

# Life in Delhi as a Supreme Court Judge

Customarily, a judge or a chief justice of a high court on being elevated to the Supreme Court is required to produce a medical certificate from the CDMO. While I was holding court at Patna towards the end of my tenure over there, I received a telephone call from the Union law minister asking me to send the necessary certificate, duly signed by the CDMO. I told the minister that unless I received such a request in writing I would not be able to get the certificate. The minister got annoyed and said that I could rely on the oral telephonic request from the minister. I made my position clear that it was not that I did not believe the telephonic request of the minister but that I would be embarrassed to ask the CDMO for a certificate without a written order from the central government. The written message did not arrive for more than 12 hours, as the fax lines were out of order. I received the fax message the next day, I again received a call from the minister. Surprised at the urgency shown by the minister, I obtained the medical certificate on priority, and sent it through a special messenger by flight but told him not to go to ministry on that day but on the day following. In the meanwhile, within only a few hours my private secretary must have received at least six calls from office of the law minister. Later on, I came to know that my colleague, the chief justice of Gujarat High Court, Justice B.N. Kripal, who was also being elevated along with me, was very keen and, in fact, was camping in Delhi at the time, and it was at his behest that the law minister was making frantic efforts to get a warrant signed as early as possible.

The notification regarding the elevation was out on 7 September 1995, and I received lots of congratulatory messages from friends and relatives. I had decided that I would spend one more week in Patna whereafter I would proceed to Delhi, but the chief justice of Gujarat High Court rang me up and personally requested me that we should take oath within a day or two. On the very next day, he again rang me up with the same request a couple of times. I told him that he, being senior, could take oath immediately, but I would take oath later on. At this, he met the CJI with the proposal, but the CJI insisted that both the judges be sworn in on same day. In the evening, therefore, my colleague rang me up again and requested me to come to Delhi as quickly as possible. I had no other alternative but to concede, and the oath ceremony was fixed for 11 September. With that end in view, I booked my passage for Delhi on the morning flight on 10 September.

The year 1995 was an eventful year in my life. In January that year my eldest son got married. In May, I was appointed as chief justice of Patna High Court. And in September 1995, hardly after a period of three months as chief justice, I was elevated as a judge of the Supreme Court of India. Thus, I came to the conclusion that my eldest daughter-in-law had brought all the luck for me.

Before leaving for Delhi, I wanted to make a courtesy call on L.N. Sharma, retired CJI. But when I rang up, he insisted that he was on his way to my residence himself. He reached within half an hour and gave me a quick lowdown on the workings of the Supreme Court and also advised me not to speak my mind freely when there. He then made me a request to see to it that three senior-most judges of Patna High Court, namely Justice B.N. Aggarwal, Justice B.P. Singh and Justice S.B. Sinha, who were competent by all means, should be elevated to Supreme Court. He also told me that he was making this request to me because the only judge from Patna in the Supreme Court would retire very soon. He reminded me that since I was the representative of Patna in the Supreme Court, it was my duty to ensure that efficient and competent judges from this state would be elevated.

I also took this opportunity to personally meet and convey my gratitude to the governor and the CM for their cooperation during my short tenure in Patna and expressed my apology for not being able to accept their dinner invitation on account of this rushed departure. I could not even accept the dinner invitation from any of the Bar associations except one official farewell lunch hosted on 9 September. While I was leaving the premises of Patna High Court after lunch, I felt as if I was leaving behind a kingdom; no such feeling had plagued me when I was leaving Orissa High Court, where I had spent a good 12 years. This is surely because of the love and affection I received from the brother judges of Patna High Court during my short tenure there. I really developed a special relationship with that high court and even after my retirement from the Supreme Court, I continue to have the same feeling towards Patna High Court.

On the morning of 10 September, my wife and I left for the airport with our total belongings packed in two suitcases. The airport was packed with the judges of Patna High Court and the members of the legal fraternity who had gathered to see me off to my new posting. I found the farewell as warm as my welcome at Patna station, which has remained in my memory ever since, as I had never experienced this in Orissa. The aircraft had a stopover at Ranchi. The brother judges at Ranchi, too, had come to the airport, and the airport manager came to the aircraft to request me and my wife to proceed to the lounge where the brother judges and their spouses had been waiting to meet me. I acceded to that request but at the same time told them that the flight should not be delayed on that count. We went to the lounge, met the brother judges and their spouses, had a cup of tea and returned to the aircraft.

On the flight to Delhi, several thoughts came to me, but the most important one was that while many judges make frantic efforts, including through political clout, to arrive at the most prestigious institution of the country on Tilak Marg, I could reach that prestigious building without any lobby, political influence or conscious effort. I came to the conclusion that this was the result of the blessings of Lord Jagannath and Lord Radhakanth Dev and the good wishes of my friends, and, finally blessings of my parents. I also realised what Shastri Babu had told me years back and thus became doubly confirmed that it was the good fortune of my wife that made it possible for me to reach the highest level of career as a judge.

When we arrived at Delhi Airport, we were received by the registrar general of the Supreme Court, Mr Chatterjee, the deputy registrar of protocol and Nisha Bhardwaj, who had been posted as my private secretary. This welcome was rather simple when compared to the one I received in Patna. From there we proceeded to Bihar Bhavan. I knew that my residential quarter would not be available at such short notice. I had, therefore, requested the CM of Orissa to make four rooms available for me at Orissa Bhavan, and so it was arranged. But when the CM of Bihar came to know about it, he insisted that I should stay at least for a week in Bihar Bhavan. Therefore, I had decided to stay in Bihar Bhavan for the first week, and from the second week onwards, I put up at Orissa Bhavan, where we spent about six–seven weeks until I was allotted the bungalow at 10, Krishna Menon Marg.

After reaching Bihar Bhavan, I immediately told my private secretary to find out the convenience of the CJI in the afternoon so that we could call on him for 10 minutes. Within 15 minutes, she informed me that the meeting was confirmed for 6 pm at the CJI's residence. When my wife and I reached 5, Krishna Menon Marg, which was the residence of CJI, I found that CJI Ahmadi and his wife were waiting for us in their living room. I expressed my gratitude and also conveyed my apology for not being able to meet him earlier. In course of the evening, the CJI gave me an idea of the workload of the judges in the Supreme Court, which hardly allowed any spare time. He also told me that even though he had met me briefly sometime in 1990, when he was in Orissa to inaugurate a state-level Lok Adalat, he remembered my face. Of course, at that point of time he was not the CJI but the executive chairman of the Legal Service Authority. He also recalled meeting me at the seminar in Ahmadabad. We spent about half an hour with him and returned to Bihar Bhavan.

Reaching Bihar Bhavan, I found that the daily list for the next day was on my table and that I was to sit with Justice Kuldeep Singh, who was the senior-most puisne judge of the Supreme Court, and, my colleague, the chief justice of Gujarat High Court, who was to take oath with me, was to sit with the CJI. Then I started going through the records of the cases scheduled for the next day. As I was regular at the Supreme Court when I was the government advocate, I had an idea as to how the cases were conducted in the court. Out of 83 briefs on my table that night, I went through about 43 and retired for the night, but I got up at 4 am and went through the rest of the briefs. I even marked some of the briefs, thus sorting out the ones that should be entertained from the ones that should not.

The next morning, after getting ready and taking breakfast, I left for the Supreme Court, where the *jamadaar* met me on the portico of the court. The judges of the Supreme Court usually meet in the coffee lounge every day, and from there proceeded to their respective courtrooms. I was, therefore, taken directly to the said lounge from my chamber. As a judge in Orissa High Court, I was not using the stiff collar, and so I did not have any stiff collar on the first day when I took oath in the Supreme Court. By the time I reached the coffee lounge, I found that there were three–four unfamiliar faces. I introduced myself to them and took my seat without knowing that in that room the judges had their marked seats mostly in order of seniority. My colleague, brother Justice B.N. Kripal, who was also due to be sworn in along with me, being a judge of Delhi High Court, had known about the stiff collar, and I saw him putting it on.

The oath-taking ceremony of a judge in the Supreme Court is a very informal ceremony. It is held in the courtroom of the CJI, and all the judges of the Supreme Court are present on the dais. That day, the entire courtroom was filled with the advocates of the court and the guests of the judge designate. The registrar general read the warrant of appointment and then the CJI administered the oath. My personal guests were my wife, my two sons, my eldest daughter-in law and a few friends of my elder son. Justice Kripal, on the other hand, had a large number of guests. The oath-taking ceremony stood concluded in 15 minutes, and afterwards the guests and the judges were served coffee in the lounge.

That day court started around noon. Even though I did not have any acquaintance with Justice Kuldeep Singh, but he being a Sardar, I had no difficulty in identifying him. We were allotted court number 2. When the court work started, he was dismissing the special leave applications one after the other, hardly spending less than a minute on a case. After the dismissal of about nine cases, I found I had marked the 10th case as fit for entertaining. So, before Justice Singh began to say anything, I started discussion and took the lead. After about five minutes, notice was issued. Out of 83 cases, only in six cases notice was issued on my insistence, otherwise probably all the cases would have been dismissed. Generally, a new judge, when he takes oath, keeps mum in the court for quite some time. But since I participated in the discussion in every case right from the first day, the members of the Bar were quite appreciative and a number of senior lawyers congratulated me and also insisted that I should express my views irrespective of what the senior judge may say.

Our court work ended by 3 pm, after which Justice Singh called me to his chamber and offered me a cup of tea. He also enquired as to whether I was a member of India International Centre (IIC). When I answered in the negative, he was kind enough to ring up the secretary of the centre to send an application form for membership of the IIC and also told him that he would require it immediately. Within half an hour, the form was sent across and he took my signature thereon and he himself became the proposer. He told me that he would get it filed after getting it seconded by another member.

I noticed that in the Supreme Court, judges were not required to sign the order sheet, and the court master issued the same after getting it vetted by the judge. In the high court, however, the judge was required to sign the order sheet himself. Later, when coffee was being served in the lounge, Justice Hansaria called me aside and kindly informed me about putting on of the stiff collar as well as about the sitting arrangement in the coffee lounge.

Thus began my strenuous life as a judge of the Supreme Court, a tenure of seven years and five months.

As my wife was due to leave for Orissa, the welcome dinner hosted by the CJI and brother judges of the court to welcome my colleague Justice B.N. Kripal and myself was fixed on Friday that week. The invitation card was issued in the name of the CJI and his companion judges. The guests included the former CJIs and their spouses, the attorney general, the solicitor general, and president and secretary of the Bar Association.

I really felt awkward when I found that on the day of the dinner that the last person to leave the Supreme Court precincts was the junior-most judge of the court, even though the dinner was being hosted in honour of welcoming two new judges. I was surprised to find that the host would leave the campus while the guests would leave at the end. I tried my best to change the system but could not succeed with the first three succeeding CJIs. When Dr A.S. Anand became the CJI—by that time I had been a Supreme Court judge for four years—I pursued the matter. Finally, he agreed and the custom was changed. The CJI and the brother judges would leave only after the invitees left the campus. But recently, when I had gone to the Supreme Court to attend a dinner held in the new building, on the occasion of retirement of a judge of the Supreme Court, I found the practice had been given a go by and the invitees like me left much later than the hosts themselves. My idea of mentioning this incident is that it is disrespectful to the guests, who usually are much older than the hosts, if the host leaves the premise even before the guests have left.

My wife left Delhi after a few days, but before her departure, she organised my relocation to Orissa Bhawan, and I continued to stay there till the allotted bungalow on 10, Krishna Menon Marg was made habitable. My younger son, Anjan, who was working in Delhi at that time was also staying with me and was occupying one of the four rooms that had been allotted in my favour. One room was being used as my office room. The third room was used as my drawing room, and the fourth one was my bedroom. Those days, after returning from the court, I used to take a stroll in the evening, but a few days thereafter, the ACP in charge of the area met me personally and advised me not to go for morning or evening walks based on an intelligence report of a terrorist attack on a VIP. Even though I did not believe in that statement, being new to Delhi, I obliged to his request.

On the second day as a Supreme Court judge, I was put on the bench with Justice K. Ramaswamy, and our bench continued roughly for a year. He was very sincere and a workaholic. Mondays and Fridays were 'miscellaneous' days, and on those days, fresh cases for admission and after-notice cases were listed. The other three weekdays were called 'regular hearing' days when cases after grant of leave and fixed for final hearing were listed. On miscellaneous days, usually most benches got up before lunch after finishing the list, whereas our court continued till 5 pm. Justice Ramaswamy would not get up until and unless the entire list was exhausted. He used to dictate order in the court, and all those orders after being typed were passed on to me in evening, and I would not only go through them but make the necessary corrections before sending it to the court master. My workload, thus, increased. But Justice Ramaswamy had given me the full authority to make whatever corrections were necessary. I remember that sometimes I even changed text, although I kept to the original decision dictated in court. Even though I had a cordial relationship with him, in several cases, I also had a difference of opinion with him and used to give deferring judgements. But he always treated me as a younger brother and even discussed his personal matters with me. He was very popular among the members of the Bar, and I remember how the Bar felicitated him on his retirement. After retirement, he left for Hyderabad, and I remained in touch with him. We used to contact each other at least twice a year. Sadly, he has been taken away from our midst by the Almighty.

While at the Supreme Court, I learnt about the unique categorisation of judges which dictated the treatment they received from the CJI and the registry office. Those judges who could be the CJI in future were in

Grade A, and consequently received the best treatment. Those judges who would become members of the collegium in due course were Grade B. Next were the judges who would have a tenure of about five years but would still retire without being members of collegium, i.e., Grade C. Last was Grade D comprising judges who were elevated just prior to their retirement and who would barely enjoy a tenure of three years in the Supreme Court. The last two categories really suffered, since neither the registry nor the CJI attached any importance to them. I was indeed surprised to learn that Justice Hansaria's request, as narrated by himself, to have a wastepaper basket in his chamber was not accepted. He then observed, 'Since you are in Grade A, you will have no difficulty.' However, there were no official papers indicating such grades, and it was only an informal way of functioning.

One other thing I observed was that usually junior colleagues did not participate in the discussion in the courtroom. Normally, it takes about three years to preside over a bench. After I started presiding over a bench, I noticed that whenever I asked the opinion of a brother judge, they would not give any response. But my temperament was just the reverse. Right from when I took oath as a judge in Orissa High Court, I participated in each and every matter right from day 1, and in the Supreme Court, too, I did the same. To me, this concept of senior judge and junior judge is ridiculous.

I also observed that the private secretaries in Supreme Court were very efficient in all protocol arrangement but not so very efficient in taking dictation when judgement was dictated, whereas the private secretaries in the high court were just the reverse. My private secretary while I was a judge in Orissa High Court, was an excellent stenographer, and when he placed the judgement for final approval after taking the dictation and getting it typed, I had never found a single mistake. In Delhi, however, I used to check the draft at least twice before pronouncing a judgement, which was dictated to my private secretary. But the court masters attached to Supreme Court were quite efficient.

Since I mentioned the strenuous life of a judge of a Supreme Court, it would be appropriate to mention a few things in that regard if only to remove people's misconception that the judges of Supreme Court enjoy too much leisure and vacation, while some even make criticism on the ground that such vacations are untenable in view of the huge pendency of cases in court. The work of a judge is completely different from the work of a bureaucrat or politician or even a common man. A judge who hears a case thinks about the same till he goes to bed, and this process of thinking is a tiring job. The workload of a judge is quite heavy in that on miscellaneous days, namely Mondays and Fridays, the list usually contains as many as 60–70 cases on Mondays and 40–50 cases on Fridays. That apart, for a newly elevated judge, it takes quite some time to adjust himself to the new environment, since the procedure adopted in the Supreme Court is slightly different than in the high courts. I used to get the miscellaneous briefs for Friday by Wednesday evening, and would spend my evenings on Wednesday and Thursday as well as some part of Friday morning to go through them. As for briefs listed on Monday, I got them by Friday evening, and spent the entire weekend reading those briefs. In addition, Tuesday Wednesday and Thursday were spent on regular hearing matters, and those matters where judgements were kept reserved required to be dealt with on Sunday mornings. Thus, a judge of the Supreme Court is hardly afforded any spare time throughout a week. But the brain requires certain respite, and it is the idea behind court vacations. I am sure the critics do not have any idea about the working of a judge, and therefore, make the criticism mindlessly.

The working method in the Supreme Court is slightly different and, therefore, any judge, howsoever brilliant, would require at least six months to get himself adjusted to the ways of the Supreme Court. I considered the senior judges with whom I sat as my teachers. I also expressed this in my farewell speech when I retired as CJI. I also imbibed different qualities from these teachers. I considered four of the senior judges as my teachers, they being Justice Kuldeep Singh, Justice K. Ramaswamy, Justice S.C. Aggarwal and Justice G.N. Ray. The skill with which Justice Singh dictated an order or judgement even after hearing big appeals deserves due respect. Justice Ramaswamy was very sincere, and one should emulate his dedication. One should learn the art of patience in hearing a matter from Justice Aggarwal. And a gentleman's dealing in courts should be learnt from Justice G.N Ray. Any judge with these qualities, utilising his own knowledge and intelligence, can be considered an able judge and will be popular and efficient. The expression 'merit should be the prime consideration for elevation to the Supreme Court' in my opinion doesn't mean only the art of judgement writing or erudition in law but should also take into account all other qualities like honesty, integrity, dealing with members of the Bar, the staff and registry, and a general reputation in society together with his seniority in the All-India list of judges.

In Delhi, the greatest advantage I found in my allotted bungalows was the existence of a number of outhouses. This was true of every quarter. I stayed for about two years in 10, Krishna Menon Marg, and another four years in 4, Motilal Nehru Marg, followed by a year in 5, Krishna Menon Marg, and in all these quarters, there existed at least a dozen staff quarters, which enabled the occupier to have people around for all jobs imaginable to run the house. Life becomes much easier for the lady of the house. To live in an apartment after retirement with only a couple of part-time house helps becomes the most difficult part in the life of a homemaker.

In May 1996, I went to Cuttack, and returned to Delhi with my daughter and wife in tow and all our belongings from Orissa. My daughter had passed her BSc Hons in Physics with First Class distinction, but chose not to continue in MSc but study for an MBA degree. Since, by the time she reached Delhi, it was too late for getting admission into an MBA degree, she joined the Indian Law Institute for a degree in Labour Law. In 1997, however, she could secure an admission into the FORE School of Management for her MBA course. All my children joined the corporate sector after obtaining their MBA degrees, and I was probably the only judge in the Supreme Court none of whose relatives, either a son or a son-in-law or a daughter, was a lawyer. It is possibly because I had never pressured on my children to choose any particular career and allowed them the freedom to decide for themselves. By God's grace, each of my children has done well in their respective careers.

When I took oath as a judge of the Supreme Court, I was the fourth person from Orissa to be elevated to the apex court. I was firmly of the opinion that many eminent judges of Orissa High Court had been ignored in the past. I also decided that before I retire in 2002, it would be my endeavour to see to it that at least one more judge from Orissa got elevated to the Supreme Court. With that end in view, after being a bit familiar with the CJI and other judges, I once met the then CJI and requested him to consider the case of the senior-most judge of Orissa High Court who by then had been elevated as the chief justice of Allahabad High Court. To my utter surprise, I got a negative response from the CJI on the ground that the even though the said friend of mine had taken an appointment from the CJI, he had not kept the appointment. That was certainly valid ground, and I could not insist the matter any further. After the CJI's retirement, when the next man was appointed in his place, I was hopeful, since I had known him from before and he was sympathetic towards me. On one occasion when I asked him why a second man from Orissa was not being elevated to the Supreme Court, the answer I got was that the next senior-most man who was continuing as chief justice of Allahabad High Court was known to not take any decision on his own and was dependent on the advice of the brother judge, and such a man, therefore, should not be brought to the Supreme Court.

My dream to see a second man form Orissa as a judge of the Supreme Court thus got thwarted. But I waited patiently for the next CJI to be sworn-in. The next man, before being appointed as CJI, faced a lot of criticism and was even quite unsure of his appointment as CJI. During that period, he had come to my house on several occasions and, in the process, I had become friendly with him. Few days after the third man was appointed as CJI, he had come to my house again, and during the conversation, I raised the topic of having a second judge from Orissa in the Supreme Court. He quietly told me that the next senior-most man from Orissa was a relation of mine, and therefore, it would not be proper to have two persons from the same family in the Supreme Court at a time. I was really surprised to learn this from him and was sure that he had been misled by some misinformation. I then replied to him that the man in question was a good friend from my college days and not any relation of mine. The CJI then assured me that he would consider his case, but it came to naught. In fact, during his tenure as CJI, there was not a single appointment of a judge in the Supreme Court. The collegium, during his tenure, did recommend four names, but the government did not agree and while there was a delay on the part of the government, a petition had been filed in the Supreme Court. Apprehending that court may take any adverse view, the government got a reference made by the president under Article 143 of the Constitution and took the stand that no appointment should be made until the reference was answered. I was a member of that bench which answered the reference. It is now known as 'Third Judges Case'. Thus, my hope of having a second man from Orissa remained unfulfilled.

Then came Dr Justice A.S. Anand. I learnt one day from my colleagues that the collegium meeting for choosing judges for being elevated to the Supreme Court would be held shortly. Determined to continue my efforts for getting a second person from Orissa in the Supreme Court, I took an appointment with CJI on Sunday and reached his residence around 11 am. He was quite friendly with me, and after some discussion, when I raised the topic as to the elevation of a second person from Orissa to the Supreme Court, he immediately replied that the senior-most Judge from Orissa, who was working as chief justice of Allahabad High Court, never wrote any judgement on his own and as such was not fit to be elevated as a judge of the Supreme Court. When I told him that all this was malicious and false, he replied that he had heard this from several lawyers and judges from Allahabad. I was surprised to find that such false rumours were being circulated. But I strongly refuted the rumours, although I noted that it was true that he was late in writing a judgement. Just then tea and snacks were served, and as I was thinking of broaching the subject again, he himself asked me to meet Justice Bharucha, who was the senior-most puisne judge in the Supreme Court. Justice Bharucha was staying in 7, Krishna Menon Marg, adjacent to 5, Krishna Menon Marg. I could guess that the CJI himself probably had no inhibition but wanted the support of his brother judge who was next in seniority to him and was poised to be the next CJI. It was about 1 pm then, and I had not taken any prior appointment from Justice Bharucha, but on the insistence of the CJI, I decided to meet him that day itself. So, I called him to secure an appointment, and he asked me to come over. When I reached his residence, he enquired about the urgency. I replied that there was no urgency but that I had come with a request.

When he probed further on the matter, I asked in reply why a second man from Orissa High Court was not being considered for elevation to the Supreme Court. Justice Bharucha was a straightforward man, and he told me that there should be no objection to having a second person from Orissa, even though Orissa High Court was a small high court. But he said that he, too, had heard the rumours about the judge in question. From this, I gathered that he had discussed this matter with the CJI earlier, otherwise the same question could not have been posed by both of them. I, however, strongly refuted that rumour as baseless. He then pointed out one rumour that my friend had heard more than 50 cases in Orissa High Court, and without delivering judgement, had left for Allahabad High Court. I knew that somebody was conspiring against my friend. I, however, replied that it may have been a couple of cases but the number 50 was wholly untrue. He then told me that since a request was being made, his name would be considered during the next meeting of the collegium, but a positive result could not be guaranteed. I replied to him that I fully trusted him, and with this word, I left his house.

On my way back, I reflected on the attitude of CJI and Justice Bharucha, and thought to myself that possibly my attempt would succeed this time. Few days thereafter, the government of India published a notification naming four judges to be elevated to the Supreme Court, and one of them was my friend, the then chief justice of Allahabad High Court. Thus, my attempt to have a second person from Orissa finally succeeded, and 48 years after the Supreme Court came into existence, there were two judges from Orissa High Court at the Supreme Court at the same time. This indicated how the judges of a small high court suffer and many such eligible persons stand ignored. Even though I had not become a member of collegium, my request to the CJI and senior-most judge in the collegium was considered, and I was happy to work with my friend as colleagues in the Supreme Court.

During my tenure of more than seven years in the Supreme Court, I was instrumental directly in the elevation of about eight judges, and indirectly, in respect of two other judges. I am using the expression 'indirectly' because even though I had expressed my opinion against them during the discussion, when the CJI wanted a written opinion from me, I had written that although I had never worked with them, from what I had gathered from the members of the Bar went to show that they were nice gentleman and popular amongst the lawyers. Written opinion was necessary because, by that time, I had not become a member of the collegium.

On the retirement of Justice N.P. Singh in December 1996, there was no judge from Patna High Court in the Supreme Court, even though earlier when the judge strength was only seven in the Supreme Court, there were three judges from Patna High Court amongst them. I became a member of collegium in 1999. Since then, when any informal discussion was underway as to which judge from Patna High Court should be elevated to the Supreme Court, one of the members of the collegium would always make a comment that the senior-most judge did not know how to write a judgement, and therefore, should not be elevated to the Supreme Court. I, thus, realised the attitude of the said judge, who was the third senior judge in the collegium.

The second senior judge from Patna High Court had a lot of influence, as he was the grandson of the former CJI and was also an advocate on record in the Supreme Court. The two other brother judges from the Supreme Court used to tell me privately that the senior-most judge from Patna High Court would be bypassed and the second senior-most judge would be brought in and I should not agree to the same. One of those two judges was also a former Chief Justice of Patna High Court. When I asked those brother judges as to how they had learnt this, the reply was that it was the gossip in the Supreme Court Bar Association, and even the lawyers in Patna knew this fact. I used to tell them that I would certainly protest against any supersession among the judges fit to be elevated to the Supreme Court from Patna. But ultimately, if the decision went otherwise in the collegium meeting, then I would not like to give anything in writing, since, in my view, both the senior-most judge of Patna and second most senior-judge were competent for being elevated to the Supreme Court. But there was no reason why the senior-most should be bypassed.

Sometime in early 2000, the question of elevation of a judge from Patna High Court came to be considered in the collegium. The meeting was being held in 5, Krishna Menon Marg, the residence of the CJI. The registry prepares a chart, which is given to each member of the collegium, that shows since when there has been no elevation from the particular High Court and who are the three senior-most judges of that High Court and their respective placements on that day. I was the fourth senior member in the collegium. Since there was no one in the Supreme Court from Patna High Court for more than three-and-a-half years, the case of that high court was taken up as the first case. Immediately, when the matter came up for consideration, the third senior-most judge in the collegium commented that the senior-most judge of Patna High Court does not write any judgement, so the second senior-most judge, then chief justice of Bombay High Court, should be elevated to the Supreme Court.

The fifth judge in the collegium, a judge from Kerala High Court, supported this and stated that a former chief justice of Patna High Court who was in the Supreme Court but had retired by then was also of the same opinion. I, however, strongly refuted the two grounds mentioned earlier and stated that the statement of the honourable members of the collegium that the senior-most judge didn't work and did not write judgement was not correct. When the fifth judge in the collegium stated that he had been advised on the matter by a judge who was the former chief justice of Patna who retired as a judge of the Supreme Court, I stated that I had also taken the views of two other judges who were the former chief justices in Patna and who were still continuing as judges of the Supreme Court, and they were of the opinion that the senior-most judge should not be bypassed. In this way, the discussion went on for more than half an hour. After that the CJI expressed his view, agreeing with the two other members of collegium. When the CJI expressed his view, I thought there was no hope for the senior-most judge for whom I was fighting, but still I didn't lose my hope and told in the meeting that the views of members of collegium were either based on hearsay or the so-called general reputation among the members of the Bar, but that I was the only judge who had the opportunity of working with both the judges in question while I was the chief justice of Patna High Court. And having taken into consideration their legal acumen, intelligence, behaviour in court towards the member of the bar, their general reputation among the public, their honesty and integrity, there was not an iota of reason for which the senior-most judge should be bypassed and the second senior-most judge be brought to Supreme Court. I also said that I would expect the members of the collegium to give due weight to my personal assessment. At this, the second senior-most judge in the collegium who had not participated throughout that meeting came out in my support. Thereafter, the CJI also had a change of heart. The two brother judges who were opposed also expressed their concurrence, and the name of the senior-most judge was unanimously conveyed to government. Finally, the notification was issued, and the said gentleman took oath as judge of the Supreme court sometime in October 2000. I felt a great sense of satisfaction that day. The senior-most judge of Patna was no friend or relation of mine but a victim of lobbying, and gross injustice would have been meted out to him, and it is for that reason, I felt it my duty to take up his cause. Few months thereafter the second senior-most judge of Patna, who was continuing as chief justice of Bombay High Court, was also elevated as a judge of the Supreme Court, and thus two-senior most members from Patna were now elevated to the Supreme Court, just as Justice L.N. Sharma had hoped.

In the meanwhile, by then, from Orissa, there were two of us in the Supreme Court, and the next senior-most judge had been elevated as chief justice of Kerala High Court. After continuing there for about 7–8 months, he was transferred as chief justice of Delhi High Court. While in Delhi, he used to visit my residence almost every afternoon on his way back home after finishing the court work, and the only thing he could talk about was as to how early he could be brought to the Supreme Court. I used to tell him that since from Orissa High Court, with a judge strength of about 14–15, when two of us were already there, it would be difficult to suggest a third name. But if any other member in the collegium suggested his name, then I would definitely support him with full force. I also told him that soon after the other judge from Orissa retired in August 2002, his case could be considered. He, however, would insist that I should try for his elevation earlier.

While this was a continuing affair, sometime in July 2001, one day during lunch hour, the CJI called me to his chamber. There, I found the second-senior most judge of the Supreme Court present; and they seemed to be discussing something. Few months prior to that, on repeated request from the President of India, a judge of Kerala High Court had taken oath as a judge of Supreme Court, and given his seniority, he was to be the CJI for about three years. The CJI and his colleague were trying to find out a strong-minded person to be brought to the Supreme Court who would be able to resist any unjust proposal from the Kerala gentleman who would be the next CJI. And they wanted my views on the same and also suggestion of such a person. I thought within myself for a while and formed an opinion that this would be an opportunity to suggest the third man's name from Orissa, which would be definitely in the interest of Orissa High Court. I prayed to Lord Jagannath and suggested his name. The second senior-most judge in the collegium inquired from me whether

I was confident about his ability and I answered in the affirmative. Finally, his name was approved by the collegium. The day his name was made known to brother judges of Supreme Court while I was entering the coffee lounge, a brother judge who was from Delhi High Court told me accusingly that I was responsible for manipulating the elevation of this third judge from Orissa. The accusatory tone in his voice hurt me then and I could not resist myself and replied, though with a smiling face, that nobody could surpass him in manipulations. And the matters stopped there. Ultimately the third judge from Orissa took oath as a judge of Supreme Court of India in October 2001.

Few days thereafter, at a dinner in Rashtrapati Bhavan, Mr Arun Jaitley, a minister in the PM's cabinet was sitting next to my wife, and posed a question to her asking if she was aware as to how many judges were there in Orissa High Court. My wife replied that she was not sure but maybe about twelve. The next question was as it how was it that from amongst them, three could be elevated to the Supreme Court. My wife kept silent and reported the exchange while we were returning home after the dinner. Thus, not only the so-called Punjabi lobby but politicians, too, were very sour when three judges from Orissa High Court were there as judges in the Supreme Court. But, unfortunately, the politicians from Orissa never expressed their resentment when there was none from Orissa High Court in the Supreme Court. As far as I know, only CM J.B. Patnaik had once, in a meeting with the then CJI, made a query as to why nobody from Orissa was getting a place in the Supreme Court, and the reply he had received was that Orissa High Court being a small one, it becomes difficult to find a suitable person. How unsustainable the views of the CJI proved when three from the said high court were judges at the Supreme Court at one point of time.

By 2002, while three of us from Orissa High Court had become judges of the Supreme Court, from Patna there were only two. The third gentleman about whom Justice Sharma had mentioned was indeed an able judge. He had been transferred to Calcutta and, by that time, had become the chief justice of Delhi High Court. My predecessor, who became the CJI, was originally from Delhi High Court. He had once sounded me about the person who was working as the chief justice of Rajasthan, desiring that he be brought to Supreme Court. By that time there were already two or three persons from Delhi who were in the Supreme Court. The gentleman in question was, in my opinion, not competent to be elevated to the Supreme Court. But the CJI told me that unless I agreed for his elevation, then the third man from Patna about whom I had told him could not be elevated. I thought to myself as to why should an able and competent person lose his opportunity, and therefore, I had to agree to the request of the CJI and both of them, namely the chief justice of Rajasthan High Court who was from Delhi and the chief justice of Delhi High Court who was from Patna, got elevated to the Supreme Court. Both of them are no more in this world. But I was finally at rest that the request of Justice L.N. Sharma could be fulfilled, and all the three judges from Patna High Court served their tenure in the Supreme Court very competently. The purpose of this account is to give an idea as to how the process of appointment of judges in the Supreme Court works.

I was really sorry when later one of the most competent and able judges of Patna High Court, Justice S.N Jha, could not be elevated to the Supreme Court. I heard that on account of political pressure, the collegium did not recommend his name. I wondered how this was possible under the collegium system, where even though the views of the CJI were given primacy, a name could be approved only when the CJI and five senior-most judges agreed on the appointment of a candidate in consideration. Perhaps the CJI or the collegium members did so in the hope of some political favours from the executive government. The able judge, mentioned above, was. Justice Jha, therefore, retired as the chief justice of Rajasthan High Court.

Later, during my tenure as CJI, in a meeting of the collegium, two names were selected after discussion for elevation to the Supreme Court. One was a judge of Allahabad High Court and the other was a judge of Madras High Court. After the decision was taken in the meeting, the same was noted on the file and the file went for signature by circulation. A few days thereafter, when I asked the confidential registrar in charge of appointment of judges as to why the file had not come for my signature till then, the answer was that the junior-most member of collegium had kept the file with him for the last four days. It was around 7 pm. I called the brother judge and asked him the reason for the delay. He said that though he had agreed in the meeting of the collegium, he was unable to agree in respect of one judge, i.e., the judge from Madras High Court because he heard something adverse against him from another brother judge from the same high court who was already in the Supreme Court. I told him that the so-called other judge from the said high court had already given in writing that the person concerned was eminently suitable for elevation to the Supreme Court. The reply I received from the brother judge in the collegium was that it was true, but the very judge who had given a 'yes' in writing had a different opinion verbally. I was really surprised and told him that he must note his disagreement based on the same to me, and I would send the file with the comment that 'you had agreed in the collegium meeting, but have changed your mind and given a different view'. Within five minutes, the file came back, and instead of any dissenting note, he agreed with the decision arrived at in the collegium meeting. This shows how judges even at the Supreme Court are sometimes unable to come to a conclusion and how such indecisions stand in the way of the dispensation of justice.

I became a judge of Supreme Court in September 1995. In October that year, the accounts officer from the registry met me and told me that my provident fund amount in my account had been transferred from Patna but not from Orissa. When I asked as to why he thought so, he replied that despite my having been a judge for more than 13 years, the provident fund account showed only Rs 45,000 in deposit, and therefore, he thought so. I told him that the figure was possibly correct, but he could not believe the same. When I insisted that the figure was correct, he immediately brought out a form and filled it himself, putting the figure of Rs 10,000 per month against provident fund deductions, and took my signature thereon. As a result, I received around more than Rs 8 lakhs from my provident fund account on my retirement. Had he not insisted, I might have continued contributing Rs 5,000 per month. I realised only on retirement how beneficial it was and thanked that officer on the day of my retirement. My financial position had never improved throughout my career as a judge. In fact, while taking tea one day, a brother judge from Andhra Pradesh advised me to even enhance the provident fund amount, but I declined, since I could not have survived with a meagre take-home salary.

Notwithstanding the fact that the salary of the judges of Supreme Court was not enough compared to the income of a busy practitioner at the Supreme Court, the life of a judge was definitely more peaceful and enjoyable. The government bungalow allocated was much spacious. Again, the facility of three LTCs per year made it possible for me to visit different places of interest within the country at minimum expenses. Even though the workload in the court was quite heavy and one hardly had any spare time, each and every vacation was being utilised to the fullest by me for visits to different places both inside and outside the country. Republic Day parade on 26 January and beating the retreat on 29 January were events I made a point to attend. In fact, the pleasure of witnessing such functions cannot be counted in money. Whenever a judge or a family member is ill, the doctor from the Supreme Court could reach your house even at midnight. If it becomes necessary to shift to any hospital, the registry takes prompt action. Even for routine check-up at the AIIMS, the specialist would come to waiting room to attend to you. Visit to places of pilgrimage become very easy. The facility of going abroad on delegation was also a great opportunity to visit countries outside India. When a judge visits some other country as a member of delegation, you get the privilege of travelling by air in first class, you are received at your destination by the embassy, accommodated in the best hotels and provided with the facilities of transport too.

I had the privilege of being the member of delegation to London in 2000 to have discussion with my British counterparts and as a member of the delegation to US Supreme Court in 2002. The visit to London in 2000 was more memorable for me since on that ticket I visited Hamburg in Germany and then from there to Rome, Florence and Venice in Italy, Vienna in Austria, where we spent three days with my intimate friend Nilamadhab who was posted as MD of UNIDO, and then to Birmingham in UK. During my visit to USA in 2002, we visited New York, Washington, Toronto, Niagara Falls, San Francisco and Hong Kong.

The year 2000 was the golden jubilee year of the Supreme Court of India. A huge amount was sanctioned by the Government of India for its celebrations. Different committees were constituted with judges of the Supreme Court as its chairmen, and I was the chairman of the exhibition committee. We collected various exhibits from different high courts of the country and placed those in the premises of the National Museum on Janpath. A replica of the Supreme Court building was also erected there. The chief justice of every high court and two other judges from each high court were invited. The exhibition continued for a month and attracted a huge crowd. After one month, a mobile train was arranged for those exhibits, and it went from one state to another all over the country. On behalf of the exhibition committee, I presented a neck tie to every judge with the emblem of the Supreme Court building on it, and their spouses were presented with a scarf. It was a landmark year in that the Supreme Court, for the first time, had full strength of judges, which was announced as an achievement by the CJI.

While at the Supreme Court, I got a chance to observe the ways of the legislative arm of the country up close. In my opinion, the age of retirement of judges of a high court and the Supreme Court should be the same. Judges with some administrative ability should be appointed as chief justices of high courts, and judges of a slightly younger age should be elevated to the Supreme Court with a minimum tenure of five years. In other words, a judge of the Supreme Court should not have more than 10 years of tenure and not less than five years of tenure. At present, only the former is followed but not the latter, and the majority of judges have a tenure of only three or four years. During my time, I had tried to persuade many of the CJIs but had failed to convince them. A judge with a tenure of three years in the Supreme Court, in my opinion, will not be able to do justice to the post, having regard to the fact that he needs some time to get adjusted to the new environment and then needs some time before retirement to make arrangements for a life after retirement. When I was a judge at the Supreme Court, I was sitting with a senior judge in the court who used to sleep in the court, and after the case got over, would ask me to dictate the order. When I visited the US Supreme Court, I noticed the same thing, as two out of nine judges were found sleeping in court. But the senior advocates who argue in the Supreme Court of India are, by and large, very learned, well-read and come fully prepared to court.

Another thing I found was that usually the chief justice and the next senior judge do not pull on well. That had been noticed by me throughout my career. Since Justice Kripal and myself took oath on the same day and both of us retired as CJI, I had decided of never creating a situation which would be grounds for dissension with the CJI. Shortly after we took oath, brother Kripal invited myself along with five other judges to his residence and was serving drinks. I did take one drink, and when he was pouring the second one, I told him that I would not like to have a second drink. In a lighter vein, he told me that one drink is offered to an enemy. I replied that he could experiment with me, and would ultimately find how untrue his statement is. On the date of his retirement, I posed the question to him in this regard, and he smiled and answered that he was indeed proven wrong. There had been no occasion for creating an inimical situation between him and myself. A very dynamic person, he became awfully busy post retirement, but, unfortunately, had a stroke and had his speech faculty impaired, undoubtedly a great infliction by the Almighty.

I continued as a puisne judge of Supreme Court from September 1995 till 10 November 2002. On 11 November, I was sworn in as the CJI. The PM was travelling and was due to be back in the county later in the day, and had made a request that I should delay the oath ceremony from the usual 10 am to 4 pm, so that he could attend the swearing-in function. But I told him that in that case, there would be no CJI from the morning till 4 pm, and it would be a very bad precedent. He immediately appreciated the matter, and the swearing-in ceremony took place in Rashtrapati Bhavan in the morning, where other dignitaries except the PM were present. Many of my close friends and relatives from Orissa came to especially attend the ceremony. I remember my cousin Jyotsna Patnaik (Kunkun) and her husband were also present. I introduced them to President Kalam, and he also recalled working with my uncle, Braja Behari, in DRDO.

Straight from the Rashtrapati Bhavan, I went to the Supreme Court and signed some files in my chambers, whereafter I took my friends and relatives to the Conference Hall where many brother judges had assembled and spent about an hour in the court. From that day till 19 December 2002, I continued as the Fourth Citizen of the country in the protocol list. That day, obviously, was the most memorable day of my life, the day when I reached the top-most post in the judicial hierarchy of our great republic. It came to my mind then that had I become a judge in 1979, I could possibly have become the CJI much earlier. But later on, I reconciled myself to my situation, thinking that Almighty gives every individual only that much that is due to him. And as such, I was supposed to be CJI for a short period. Even though I was the fourth person in the protocol list, in every function in Rashtrapati Bhavan, particularly when dignitaries from the foreign countries were on a visit, my wife got the privilege of being introduced as the first lady of the country, since the PM and the President at that time were both unmarried.

I had noticed earlier that during the swearing-in ceremony of the CJI the CM of the state to which the new CJI belongs attends the function. For example, when Justice Verma took oath, the CM of Madhya Pradesh was present. When Dr Anand took oath, the CM of Jammu and Kashmir was present, and when my predecessor took oath, the CM of Delhi was present. But when I took oath, the CM of Orissa did not attend, although the former CM of Orissa was present. I thought then that maybe the political heads of Orissa do not consider the achievement of an Odia to be of any consequence and as such do not attach any importance to it.

I arranged a lunch at my residence on the day of my swearing-in ceremony, particularly for my relatives and friends who had come from Orissa. A couple of former colleagues in the Supreme Court and sitting judges were also in attendance. In the evening, the president of India hosted a dinner in honour of the outgoing and the incoming CJI, and I had the privilege of sitting beside the president. On the dinner table, the president asked me whether I was aware of what was going on in the different high courts. I did not have any news of importance from any of the high courts. But then I learnt from the president himself that three judges of Karnataka High Court were guilty of misconduct in some resort in Mysore, and there was the allegation of some sex scandal against them. The president requested me to suspend the said judges, but I replied that I did not have that power. Then he told me that their salary should be stopped, to which I replied that I did not have that power either. At last, he said, 'Whatever power you have, exercise that and act promptly.' I returned home from dinner plagued with a great sense of shock, since on the very first day as CJI, such a scandal had arisen. I immediately contacted three brother judges from Karnataka High Court who were then my colleagues in the Supreme Court. All three of them told me that they had heard the news and there might indeed be some truth in the same.

The next morning, I called the chief secretary of Karnataka and requested him to get an enquiry underway discreetly and send me the report confidentially, but no action was taken by him, even though he had promised to send the report soon. I then thought of taking the help of the chief of the Intelligence Bureau, and met the director at my residence. He initially agreed, but a day later, he met me and told me that the then home minister, Mr L.K. Advani, did not permit him to enquire into the matter. It so happened that I accidently met the home minister at Rashtrapati Bhavan and directly confronted him on the matter. He replied that if I wanted, he could ask the CBI to hold the enquiry and submit a report. I had no confidence in the CBI's fairness in enquiry, as I was of the opinion that the CBI works under the political pressure of executive government and so it may not be proper to take their assistance. Having failed to get any such report, I decided to get the matter enquired into by a committee of three judges, comprising chief justices of two high courts and a judge of Orissa High Court, to decide as to what should be done if some allegation of misconduct is made against a judge of a high court or the Supreme Court. But to my chagrin, the committee was inefficient and had not started its job until the date of my retirement. After my retirement, the committee submitted a report exonerating the judges involved.

During my short tenure as CJI, I received allegations of misconduct against a judge of Rajasthan High Court as well as against two judges of Punjab High Court. I did constitute two such committees, and on the basis of their findings, the judge of Rajasthan High Court took retirement, and in the case of Punjab, one of the judges took voluntarily retirement, and the other judge was reprimanded and cautioned. I do not know whether any such enquiry is being conducted today. My successor was of the view that by holding such enquiries the judiciary was being maligned and hence it should be stopped. I was, all along, of the view that if such allegations are swept under the carpet, then one day it will necessarily reach a flashpoint, leading people to think that instead of taking any action, those at the helm of the affairs are facilitating the same. The only action of this nature contemplated under the Constitution being impeachment, and, the procedure for impeachment being quite difficult, though not impossible, it had been provided only to hold such enquiry and take some prompt action.

Whenever the head of any country visits India, and the president of India hosts a dinner in his honour, the CJI along with his wife are invited along with other dignitaries of the country. Such visits were so frequent in my short tenure that I must have visited the Rashtrapati Bhavan at least five–six times. Once the Russian President Vladimir Putin had been invited, but since I had already accepted an invitation from a senior member of the Bar, I had to decline the dinner invitation at Rashtrapati Bhavan. My wife, however, had argued with me that attending the dinner at Rashtrapati Bhavan in honour of president of another country was my constitutional obligation and I should not have declined the invitation on any score. I had told her then and I am still of that opinion that if I have accepted one invitation earlier, I should not cancel that merely because a dinner invitation comes much later from the Rashtrapati Bhavan. In a lighter vein, I had told her that in her absence there would be no first lady of the country on that night.

The CJI gets a lot of pressure from brother judges, mostly in matters of appointment, and to such an extent that sometimes it becomes impossible to maintain mental peace. I remember an instance involving the Himachal Pradesh High Court. The chief justice of the high court was retiring, and, since the collegium had not decided as to who would go there as chief justice next, the senior-most judge would have been notified as the acting chief justice. But about six or seven judges from the Supreme Court met me and told me that the senior-most judge should not be made the acting chief justice. I really could not understand why they were insisting on the same, nevertheless I thought that their opinion should be given due weight. I, therefore, requested the chief justice of Jharkhand High Court to meet me immediately. When he met me in the evening, I asked him whether he would have any objection if he was transferred and posted as chief justice of Himachal High Court. Initially, he was a bit unwilling but when I told him that the exigency of services required this and it would be a great favour to me, he immediately agreed and gave it in writing then and there that he had no objection to being posted as the chief justice of Himachal High Court.

Very often members of the Bar from different high courts meet the CJI with their grievances. Even though the demand may not be acceptable, a patient ear is called for. Disposal of cases in the court, appointment of judges and filling up of the vacancies in the high court and Supreme Court after taking decision in the collegium meeting, transfer of judges from one high court to another, the functioning of registry itself, discussion with the law minister and, above all, the day-to-day court work, which is usually very heavy, are the multifarious duties required to be discharged by the CJI. That apart, the CJI as the head of the 'judicial family' in the country has the responsibility to oversee well-being of the family from all angles. In a vast country like India, the duties and responsibilities of the CJI are undoubtedly very onerous, and therefore, every CJI anxiously awaits his date of retirement. So long as one continues as the CJI, I am sure that every night while going to bed he must be offering a prayer for the smooth functioning of the judiciary during his tenure. I was also looking forward to 19 December 2002. In a matter of weeks, that day arrived, and the new CJI was sworn in. That day I felt as if a heavy load was lifted off my shoulders.

The day I retired, I was quite sure about one thing, namely that hence forward there would be at least one judge from Orissa High Court in the Supreme Court, given there were three judges from Orissa at the time. But my happiness was short-lived. In the last three–four years, there had been no judge from Orissa in the Supreme Court even though the strength of the Supreme Court has been enhanced to 34 now.

Narration of life as judge of Supreme Court would remain incomplete without the mention of the supporting staff. Any person not accustomed to life in Delhi will be unable to manage the affair without the help and support of a person who is acquainted with life in Delhi. This part is played by the private secretary attached to the judge. Nisha Bharadwaj, who was there at the airport when I arrived from Patna to welcome my wife and me, continued as my private secretary till my retirement from the Supreme Court. Even though another PPS in the rank of joint registrar became attached to me on my appointment as CJI, Nisha continued to work for me. She was a very helpful hand, and discharged all that was required, starting from receiving guests at Delhi airport, even if the flights arrived at midnight, to attending to personal needs of the family members. She became a part of the family and continues to be so even today. Not only she but her family members, husband Kamal, who was working in the Home Ministry in the government of India, and their two children, son Jatin and daughter Dolly, also became quite familiar with us and remain so even today. It will be not be an exaggeration if I mention that but for her it would have been difficult for me to fulfil my duties during the period of seven-and-a-half years in the Supreme Court. In addition to attending to the personal needs of the family, she was managing the confidential matters relating to court and was also taking dictation for delivering of judgement. I had also one personal assistant named Hemant, who was essentially engaged in taking dictation and typing out the judgement. As far as other helps are concerned, I had employed one person from Orissa named Ajay, who was in charge of our kitchen and store. His duty hours started from 7 am in the morning, with him serving us tea, and ended at 10 pm in the night when we used to go to bed after dinner. He was a sincere and devoted person and is still in touch with us. There were quite a few other people who were instrumental in making life easy in a place like Delhi for me, my wife and two children, one of whom was still studying.

# Life of a Senior Citizen

On 19 December 2002, I got a four-letter suffix added to my name: Retd. With this suffix, my situation changed abruptly and drastically. Even on that very night when the brother judges host a dinner in honour of the retiring CJI, and even though the new CJI is to take oath at 10 am next day, by the time the dinner gets over, the name of the retiring CJI vanishes from the nameplate in front of the chamber of the CJI, replaced by the nameplate bearing the name of the incoming CJI. I do not know under whose order the registry takes this step. It could be possibly due to a desire to show allegiance to the incoming CJI. Almost in an instant, the behaviour of Supreme Court staff also changes. But if any judge has treated the staff well during his time in office, then those staff remain warm towards him.

Fortunately, I had very cordial relationship with the staff of the Supreme Court right from the day I took oath till the day I retired as CJI, and consequently, even after 20 years of my retirement, I have not found any change in the behaviour of the staff. The CJI, who is seated by the side of president of India at the dinner table, after retirement, gets consigned to the end of the table. This is unlike what happens to former presidents or former PMs of the country. I have not attended any dinner at Rashtrapati Bhawan after my retirement. It is in this context a question arises: if in a democracy the three pillars perform their respective duties, namely executive with the president as its head, the legislature the PM as its head and the judiciary CJI as its head, then why is it that in the matter of getting facilities after retirement the judicial head is grossly discriminated against? The privileges attached to the post are not under the Constitution but only by executive order or rules framed for the purpose. The Parliament or the executive head have never thought over this matter. After my retirement, very often while I return from my morning walk, carrying a packet of milk in my hand, I ask myself why is it that I am carrying milk from the booth. The citizens of the country are probably under a misconception that a retired CJI gets the same privileges and facilities as a retired president or PM. In fact, once when a press reporter had questioned me as to why I was staying in a rented house, I had answered that after retirement the government does not provide any accommodation to people like me.

A retired CJI is permitted to retain the government quarters for one month. I had initially decided to go back to my Bhubaneswar house and settle down there. Since my son and daughter were still unmarried and staying with me on account of their jobs in Delhi, I tried to find out a suitable apartment for them within their affordance before I could move back to Odisha, but it was impossible to get such an accommodation. My wife and I, therefore, decided that we would continue for some time by taking an apartment on rent and, accordingly, the search for a house was on. But since the time of one month to vacate the bungalow was going to expire soon, I, therefore, requested my successor that I may be allowed to continue in 5, Krishna Menon Marg for one more month on payment of rent. Having searched at different localities, my wife finally zeroed in on a four-bedroom apartment in New Friends Colony. The owner was staying on the ground floor and had rented out the first floor to us. The apartment was quite spacious, and the living room quite big. That apart, the staff's quarter was also quite big, by Delhi standards. Since we decided that our stay in Delhi would be for a short period, accordingly, we split our furniture, the major portion of which was sent back in a truck to our house in Bhubaneswar, and only a small portion was brought to New Friends Colony. Though I had requested and my successor had also agreed that I could stay in 5, Krishna Menon Marg one more month, I actually stayed there for about another 15 days before shifting to New Friends Colony. But the Supreme Court car, the entire staff, including the private secretary and the security people, continued with us for full one month even after we shifted to New Friends Colony. I searched for a domestic help who could cook in our house. A friend of mine, who was then a judge in Patna High Court, recommended a boy who knew a bit of cooking, and he joined us in our New Friends Colony house. The cleaning of house and the cleaning of utensils could be managed with part-time help. I did not have a car, so I was availing my son's car for quite some time. But we needed the air-conditioner and refrigerator, etc. While purchasing them, I was quite conscious about my monthly budget.

Then I thought of paying a short visit to Orissa. There, I stayed at the high court guest house in Cuttack. The high court staff and the vehicle were there with me. I met my relatives and friends at Cuttack and Bhubaneswar. I visited Puri for a *darshan* of Lord Jagannath. I also visited my village and prayed before our family deity. The then chief justice of Orissa High Court met me in the court guest house. While I was in the guest house, a lawyer from the Bhubaneswar Bar also met me, and in course of our conversation, told me that a judge from Orissa High Court in the Supreme Court had come to Orissa and was telling him that he would have become the CJI if it were not for my preventing his elevation to the Supreme Court for some time. I was really shocked to hear this from him, and I told the lawyer that had he been considered for the post of the CJI there was no reason for me to stop him from being elevated earlier. After the lawyer left, I thought to myself how ungrateful the gentleman was. Since at every stage of his career, including the elevation to the Supreme Court, he had sought my help and I had ungrudgingly extended help on every occasion. I consoled myself by thinking that probably this was the way of expressing gratitude of a fellow Odia. I became so much perturbed with the matter that soon after I reached my New Friends Colony residence, I rang up the gentleman and requested him to come to my residence. He did oblige and reached my house within half an hour, whereafter I gave him a piece of my mind and confronted him with the version the lawyer in Orissa had told me. He simply cried and told me how could I believe the lawyer. I replied that lawyer had no reason to fabricate a story, particularly in relation to appointment of judges to the Supreme Court. I also thought about another judge from Patna High Court who could be elevated because of my insistence even though three members of the collegium were against him. I told him that it was his luck and destiny and I had no role to play.

Two other judges, one from Madras and another from Allahabad, who were selected while I was the CJI, express their gratitude whenever they meet me even today. I compare the attitude and behaviour of my brother Odia judge and brother judges from other high courts. The former successfully prevented another Odia judge from being elevated to the Supreme Court, who was later elevated only after the retirement of the said judge who was against him and, as a result, could not become the CJI. This is an instance of how people from different parts of the country behave and work.

While I was quite apprehensive as to how it would be possible to live in Delhi with a meagre pension, in 2003, I gave opinion in about eight matters and was appointed as an arbitrator in one arbitration dispute and thus earned substantially. I came to form an opinion that it would not be difficult to manage affairs in Delhi. Retired judges of the Supreme Court have two ways of earning money after retirement, apart from the pension they receive. One is by giving opinion sought for by different litigants in any pending dispute, and the second is by becoming an arbitrator in an arbitral dispute. But I was not concerned with the same while retiring, as I had received a message from the office of the PM that I may be appointed as the chairman of the National Human Rights Commission. Under the statute, only a former CJI can be the chairman. The then chairman, who was retiring in early 2003, had himself told me that I was being appointed. Another CJI, who had retired about one-and-a-half years before me, was anxious to be the chairman, but there were several allegations against him, and the former law minister in the Government of India had written an open letter to the PM in his disfavour. Thus, he was not likely to be appointed. But he had a very powerful political lobby. The Punjabi lobby, Rajput lobby and Kashmir lobby all put their strengths behind him, and at last, even though the PM himself was not very keen to appoint him, he was appointed as chairman of National Human Rights Commission. This shows how even a person with a tarnished image can be appointed to an important post if he has the required political backing. But a man from Odisha can count on no such favour.

Disgusted with the scenario relating to the appointment to the National Human Rights Commission and somewhat upset, I decided to leave for Germany alone to visit my elder son for some time, as my wife could not accompany me on account of my second son, who was staying with us and was unwell at that time. I enjoyed my stay in the city of Hamburg in Germany and had a good time with my two grandchildren. After a week's stay there, my son and I made a visit to Moscow and St. Petersburg in Russia with a group of German tourists. Moscow gave me the impression of a huge city and every public building or institution was oversized. The weather was fine and by that time the country had accepted *perestorica*, i.e., making the country open. In other words, the so-called confinement of a communist regime was not there. The people had become more westernised than their counterparts in Western countries, both with regards to their dress and food. The famous McDonalds restaurant could be spotted in every street corner, but most of the people were unable to express in English. We had engaged a young girl as our guide, and she was quite fluent in English and so there was no difficulty in moving around in Moscow. Though we had taken the trip with a group of Germans, both in Moscow as well as in St. Petersburg, we visited the different places of interest on our own. I liked the city of St. Petersburg much more than the city of Moscow. We came back to Hamburg, and after spending about two months, I returned to Delhi in July. After my return, I took up another place in New Friends Colony for my office and started working from there. New Friends Colony is a nice colony but is a congested one, but the one advantage is the nearby Ashoka Park, where I used to take my morning walks, and my office was at a walking distance. Gradually, I got more opinion matters and more arbitration cases and earned enough to have a comfortable living.

Towards the end of 2003, Anjan, my second son went back to Orissa, and in June 2004, he got married to Sushree, the youngest daughter of Shailoja Shankar Singh Deo, belonging to the royal family of Dhenkanal. Shailoja was an engineer from IIT Kharagpur and earned his master's degree from the US. After his marriage, he chose to start his own business and started with a steel factory called IPI Steel at Dhenkanal. He thereafter set up an engineering college at Dhenkanal. He has finally left all those businesses and is now retired and residing at his house in Cuttack. For the wedding, we were in Orissa for two weeks and were staying in our Lewis Road house, which my tenants had vacated during that period. After the marriage we came back to Delhi, leaving my son and daughter-in-law in Orissa.

My daughter got married during the next year in June. She married Mahesh, son of Dilip Misra and Swarna Misra. Dilip Misra was the traffic manager at Paradeep Port and was an affable person. We had made several plans of spending time together on my permanent return to Orissa. But it never materialised, as Dilip Misra passed away in June 2006. He is survived by his wife, Swarna, who is quite well-known in the Bhubaneswar circle for her exemplary social work. She runs an institution called Susrusha that trains girls in patient care and stations them with old and invalid persons as caregivers. My daughter Rinku is presently managing director of a market research company called Ipsos in Delhi, while my son-in-law Mahesh is working as the CEO of a company called IMGC (Indian Mortgage Guarantee Corporation).

In 2006, I began to think of acquiring an apartment in Delhi, but the cost of an apartment of over a 500 sq. yard plot in south Delhi was quite high, and I did not have that much savings. My son Amar told me that if a suitable house was finally chosen, he could contribute half of the expenses, and therefore, our house search was taken up seriously and vigorously. Needless to mention, it was my wife who was visiting different parts of Delhi to look for a suitable house, and finally, we chose an apartment in Soami Nagar South. After entering into an agreement of sale by paying advance, I approached some banks to take a loan but banks refused to grant me loan on grounds of my advanced age. But luckily, around that time, I got engagement in one arbitration case and earned enough money. Finally in September 2008, our apartment in Soami Nagar South was purchased and we shifted to the same after a small puja. Though initially I had decided to continue in Delhi for a short period, after the marriage of my son and daughter, while they left Delhi, my wife and I stayed back. I must indicate that the purchase of apartment at Soami Nagar, the marriage of my son at Cuttack and the marriage of my daughter at Bhubaneswar could all be possible because of untiring efforts of my wife.

When we purchased the apartment in 2008, I had exhausted all my savings. But soon thereafter my earnings from arbitration cases as well as giving opinions grew, and within two years, I had enough funds with me. With that, I started the construction of house in Noida, where I had obtained a plot in the Allahabad High Court Judges Society. In fact, I had purchased a land on persuasion of a brother judge by paying instalment from the Provident Fund amount that I had received on my retirement. It took about three years for the completion of the house, but we never stayed in that sprawling bungalow except for the night after the puja. It was then put on rent for about four years. Thereafter the house remained vacant for quite some time and it became expensive to maintain. None of my children were interested, and finally I sold the same in 2022.

While I was a sitting judge at the Supreme Court, I had applied for a plot of land in the newly developed area of Cuttack and had been allotted a plot in Sector 11. I had taken possession of the same but had not started any construction. Many retired judges of Orissa High Court had got their land in same locality and had built their houses and were living there. In fact, the area is popularly known as Judges Area. I suddenly received a notice from Cuttack Development Authority that the period for construction of land would expire soon and unless a house was built, the land would get forfeited. After my retirement from the Supreme court, whenever I was visiting Cuttack, my hometown, I used to stay in the high court guest house. I thought to myself that if I get my house completed in CDA Cuttack, then I would not have to stay in guest house. At the same time, I could have my house of own. The joint family house was being occupied by my brother on ground floor and the first floor had been put up on rent. There was no scarcity of funds, as the pension I was drawing in Bhubaneswar was not being spent, and so also the house rent I was getting from my Lewis Road house at Bhubaneswar. It took about one-and-a-half year for the completion of our two-storey house there. My younger son,

Anjan, who was staying with his wife and son Devansh in a rented house, didn't agree to occupy the house in CDA initially. But for last five–six years, they have taken up residence at the house. Anjan after his MBA degree from XIM Bhubaneswar was working in the corporate sector and had been posted as chief project officer of a road infrastructure company called Shri Jagannath Expressway in Odisha but then left that job and is trying to establish a business of his own. Surprisingly, while in service, I had constructed only one house at Lewis Road in Bhubaneswar. However, after retirement I became the owner of one apartment in Delhi, a house in Noida and another house in CDA Cuttack.

Ever since my retirement, visits to my elder son in Hamburg in Germany became as frequent as every year or every alternate year. Amar is a managing director and global head for a Tata Group company. His wife, Michelle, a Roman Catholic with roots in Goa and Bombay, was a banker by profession but is now a homemaker. Her parents, Cyprian and Ramona were originally from Goa, but they were settled in Bombay. Cyprian was in the corporate sector and is no longer alive, but his wife Ramona, a retired headmistress, continues to live in Bombay. Amar and Michelle have two sons, his eldest son, Aaryamaan, has started working in a private equity firm in Switzerland after his master's degree in Economics from Warwick University. His second son, Ayushman, has finished his Economics Honours from Warwick too and has joined Bank of England in London. With them, we visited different countries such as Croatia, Spain, Portugal, Italy a number of times, South of France, Australia and New Zealand, Hungary, Switzerland, Greece, etc. When I visit any foreign country, I am reminded of the astrologer who had once told me that I possibly had no chance of visiting a foreign country, though by now I have visited about 40 plus countries outside India.

Disputes between the parties are usually settled in civil courts or criminal courts, but since litigation in courts take unusually long time, the legislature devised the forum of arbitration as an alternate dispute resolution organ. It was invoked in this country during British rule by the enactment of Arbitration Act of 1940, but even prior to that, the tradition of disputes being settled through a body called panchayat in India was also in vogue. Under the provision of Arbitration Act, a dispute can be resolved through a single arbitrator or a tribunal of three members, where each party would nominate their arbitrator and two nominated arbitrators choose a third one to be the presiding arbitrator. In case of tribunal, a major verdict of two arbitrators forms the award to be enforced in court of law. Since my retirement, I have been arbitrator in about 50 cases, out of which the court engagement has been five, and the party nomination about eight, the rest being my work as the presiding arbitrator on being chosen by the two arbitrators nominated by both parties. My colleagues in Delhi as well as in Bombay have got themselves busy in arbitration matters so much that they are even busier now than they were in courts. But I have never been that busy with arbitration, as it never appeared to be interesting. I derive pleasure in giving opinions though. Till about 2018, I must have given opinion every year in about 14–20 matters, and so far as arbitration is concerned, I was keeping myself busy for about 12–14 days a month at the maximum. On account of arbitration disputes, I had to visit Bombay, Calcutta, Bangalore and Ahmedabad, and apart from the money it brought in, it was quite a refreshing change for me and very relaxing. For the last two years, and particularly after the outbreak of Covid, I have hardly had a few arbitration cases, but with my long associations with the arbitrations, I can say that the purpose and object of the act has not been achieved, and the arbitration and time for completion of it has not been in anyway shorter than the time that is consumed in a court of law. The Parliament is quite serious and has brought so many amendments to ensure that the Act must be enforced in true spirit. There has been lots of improvement made by such amendments, but unless and until the lawyers for the parties who appear before the arbitral tribunal and the arbitrators themselves change their mindset, the purpose of the Act will not be served. Every commercial dispute requires early resolution, and therefore, in many advanced countries such dispute gets resolved through the process of mediation or conciliation in the shortest possible time. But in our country, though there has been a lot of improvement, things are still far from satisfactory and it still is taking considerable time for resolution of dispute through arbitration.

After my retirement, apart from keeping myself engaged in arbitration and giving opinion, I was also associated with a few other organisations. One such engagement was as the chairman of the 'Chayan Parishad' or jury for Saraswati Samman award, established by the K.K. Birla Foundation. The job of the jury, comprising a group of seven–eight literary figures from different parts of the country, is to consider the work of different literary figures, which are selected by the regional bodies, so as to decide which writer is adjudged to be best to be awarded the *samman*. The jury is the final authority to decide the writer who will be awarded. The prize money is more than Rs 7 lakh. Apart from a recognition in the literary field at the national level, that was a great opportunity for me to learn about literature, but the job was arduous. Nevertheless, I was enjoying it. Under the rule of the award committee, the translated version of every piece that comes from different parts of the country is circulated to every member of jury, and in the final meeting, the decision is taken. I was the chairman of jury for about seven years, and thereafter I myself requested the Birla Foundation to choose some younger person, as I felt the work to be quite taxing. In course of the decision-making, no doubt, initially the member of jury tries to push the author or the script from their own language, but ultimately, a decision is taken unanimously, and during my tenure as the chairman, every time the jury has given its verdict unanimously. Since I was not a literary figure and did not have much connection with literature, I found the job to be difficult but nevertheless quite interesting. Mr K.K. Birla himself was chairman of the foundation till his death, and after his death, his daughter Shobhana Bhartia became the chairman. But at no point of time, has the chairman ever tried to influence the members in giving the decision. In the literary field, the Saraswati Samaan is considered to be of the same level as Jnanpith Award. Some even consider the Saraswati Samaan to be of a higher level.

I was also part of a forum called Orissa Forum, which was founded by the famous artist Jatin Das. The Odia brotherhood are members of the said forum. It is, in fact, the thinkers' forum where every month some topic relating to the state of Orissa is discussed and some decision is taken. The topic of discussion is chosen usually by the president of the forum, and he also chooses the person who would give the talk on the subject. For quite some time, Gokul Patnaik, a former IAS, has been its president, and during his tenure, the forum is quite active. We discuss on a variety of subjects ranging from Odia literature to theatre or any current topic concerning the future of Orissa. I usually attend the meeting if I am present in Delhi and, in fact, I once told Mr Gokul Patnaik in a lighter vein that he should continue as the forum's permanent president. The institution also recognises the merit of Odias not only within the country but also outside, and there is a jury that decides the person to be awarded. I am the chairman of the said jury, and I like the work very much.

As a retired CJI, I also receive quite a few invitations from different high courts or other legal institutions to deliver lectures. Delivering a lecture, however, needs lots of preparation, and of late I decline. However, when there is an invitation from Orissa for releasing a book or addressing the students of any law university or a memorial lecture in honour of some deceased lawyer of the state, I always accept.

On 19 December 2017, I turned 80. Since my childhood my parents had never organised any celebration for my birthday. I also did not celebrate my 80th birthday. But 10 days thereafter, on 29 December, I organised a get-together of my relatives, the Das family of Ghorodia, and my intimate circle of friends and their family members as well as some close friends of my children. It was arranged at Hotel Mayfair in Bhubaneswar, and my daughter took the trouble of making the entire arrangement, starting from reservation of rooms for our guests to the menu that would be served. My close friend Mr Kula Mishra came from the US, and my sister-in-law Dr Ira Das, consultant microbiologist and her husband Dr B.N. Das, consultant ophthalmologist from Birmingham and their son Devashish and his family had come from the UK, as well as my eldest son from Germany also came. We had a congregation of about 350 people, and while I left the venue at midnight, my children continued dancing till the early hours of the morning.

On 30 December, a picnic was also organised at a scenic place called Baliharchandi on the way to Bramhagiri. On one side is the river and on the other side is the sea. My wife's cousin, Kishore (Babuli), who was then managing director of Gammon India, took the burden of making the entire arrangements for the picnic. New Year's Eve was spent in the Golf Club, where my daughter's mother-in-law Swarna and my niece's in-laws, Rashmi and Santosh Mahapatra, were present. Thus 2017 went off smoothly, and by God's grace, my health condition was very good.

Apart from these engagements, travel has been a constant of my retired life, accompanied by my kids and their families or my wife. The list of places abroad expanded to include Dubai, China, Thailand, Muscat, New Zealand, Australia, Sri Lanka, Switzerland and Japan. And it was in in April 2019, one morning while out looking for a restaurant in Kyoto in Japan, I fell in a ditch, which was quite deep and without barricade, and got injured, resulting in profuse bleeding from my eye. I could not get out by myself, though I had not lost my consciousness. The hotel staff helped me by lifting me from the ditch, but since the bleeding did not stop, we decided to go to a hospital for emergency treatment. After an MRI, satisfied that there had been no injury in the neck or head, they permitted me to leave the hospital after two hours. I was advised not to travel by car and instead rest in the hotel that day. Incidentally, my brother-in-law Tikan was with us along with his wife, and he gave me the moral support and strength of mind. As a result, I did not feel too low about the accident, even though it was a foreign land.

The rest of 2019 was utilised by me in writing several awards in arbitration matters where hearing had been completed. In the early part of 2020, both in January and February, I made several trips to Odisha particularly to attend several marriage functions of my relatives. On 10 April 2020 my second son, who lives in Cuttack, was celebrating his 50th birthday, and we had booked our air ticket to visit Cuttack on 8 April, but on 25 March on account of dire calamity posed by Covid-19, lockdown was declared, and consequently, our visit to Cuttack in April had to be cancelled.

That year, I had planned to attend the graduation ceremony of my grandson and, accordingly, booked my trip to Germany. We had planned to leave Delhi on 29 May and return on 12 July after visiting Hamburg in Germany, London in UK and Stockholm in Sweden. But the entire plan was foiled, and tickets and hotel bookings were cancelled. Right from March till end of November 2020, the time was spent within the four corners of our apartment in Soami Nagar South. Except for taking a morning walk there was no physical or mental exercise to be done. The only relaxation was playing cards with my wife for an hour at night. I utilised the time fully by writing my autobiography in Odia, which was published and released in Cuttack in 2021.

Notwithstanding the Covid-19 pandemic, the 20 years of my retired life has been spent quite peacefully. Ever since 2020, much change has been seen in our country. My arbitration assignments have practically become nil, but I still maintain my office in New Friends Colony, where I go at least three times a week. The inflation in the country has risen exorbitantly and so also the problem of unemployment. The market price has become so high that even I feel the pinch, though I do not visit the market so often. I also have a feeling that there has been erosion of institutional credibility, be it the Enforcement Directorate or CBI or CVC or even highest court of the land. A high-powered organisation, Lokpal, been set up, but during the four-year period of its existence, it has done very little. Members of the Lokpal have resigned, and there has been no appointment of chairman, who should be a retired CJI or a retired judge of the Supreme Court of India.

While the institution of Human Rights Commission at the national level as well as in the state level does exist, but I do not know to what extent they have been discharging their duties in disposing of the so-called Human Rights violation cases that are brought to their notice. As a common man, I feel disturbed with the growing intolerance in the country. On the one hand, I feel proud that our country has been able to send the Chandrayan to the moon like other developed countries of the world and is being considered as the first developing nation in the international market, with the predication that India will be the third economic power next to United States and China. On the other hand, I am upset when I find that in the sphere of providing healthcare facility, good education and reasonable housing for the common man, it is much below the standard of any other developed country in the world. When I visit Germany almost every year the only thought that comes to my mind is why has our country not been able to achieve the standard in education, health and housing for common man like in Germany, which had been devastated by the World War II in 1945 and has since been rebuilt successfully. We Indians gained independence in 1948, and although we have moved forward as a free nation since, our progress has not been comparatively satisfactory. Of late we find hate speech from high functionaries in newspapers. In one of the recent judgements, the Supreme Court of India has observed, 'Public Functionary and other person of influence and celebrity, having regard to their real and apparent authority and impact they will on public and certain section thereof owe a duty to the citizenry at large to be more responsible and restrained in their speech.' But such observation has not had any visible impact. While in school I had read a poem titled "Where the Mind is without Fear"—the poem was a self-translation of one the Bengali poems by the famous poet Rabindranath Tagore published in the collection *Geetanjali*. The last few lines of the poem which I still remember are:

*Where the clear stream of reason has not lost its way*
*Into the dreary desert sand of dead habit*
*Where the mind is led forward by thee*
*Into ever-widening thought and action*
*Into that heaven of freedom, my Father, let my country awake.*

I pray to the Almighty to take our country to that level of freedom and fearlessness that the Nobel laureate had thought and expressed in the aforesaid song.

*Deity of Lord Radhakanta Dev in Ghorodia village*

*Ghorodia Upper Primary School, where the author studied for two years, 1942–43*

*The author's father and mother with their three grandchildren Amar, Anjan and Rinku*

*The author along with his colleagues from the Supreme Court of India in Washington with Justice Sandra Day O'Connor of US Supreme Court during their visit as part of India's delegation in October 2002*

*(From L–R): Author with his brother and sisters—Younger brother Janaki Ballav, youngest sister Himanshu Bala, eldest sister Sudhanshu Bala and author Gopal Ballav*

*Photograph of the author after being sworn-in as CJI with (L–R) Law Minister Jana Krishnamurthy, author, Vice President Bhairon Singh Shekhawat, President A.P.J. Abdul Kalam, Deputy Prime Minister L.K. Advani, Justice B.N. Kirpal (preceding CJI of India)*

*Author's family in December 2017 on the occasion of his 80th birthday*

*The author receiving the Utkal Ratna Award from Utkal Sathiya Samaj, the oldest literary institution of Odisha, in March 2021*

*President Kalam administering oath to the author as CJI in Ashoka Hall, Rashtrapati Bhavan*

*The author with President A.P.J. Kalam and colleagues Justice Rajendra Babu and Justice M.B. Shah at the Supreme Court during the president's visit and discussion with the Supreme Court judges*

*The author in his office in the Supreme Court chamber as Chief Justice of India*

*The author and his wife with President Droupadi Murmu in Rashtrapati Bhavan*